HISTORICAL HEROES

HISTORICAL HEROES

By
Mick Gowar
Dennis Hamley
Martin Oliver
Victoria Parker

Miles Kelly

First published in 2010 by Miles Kelly Publishing Ltd
Harding's Barn, Bardfield End Green, Thaxted, Essex, CM6 3PX, UK

This edition printed 2014

6 8 10 9 7 5

Publishing Director Belinda Gallagher
Creative Director Jo Cowan
Additional Design Kayleigh Allen, Joe Jones
Line Art Illustrator Mike Mosedale
Production Manager Elizabeth Collins
Reprographics Anthony Cambray, Stephan Davis, Ian Paulyn
Assets Lorraine King

Authors Napoleon, Julius Caesar: Mick Gowar
William Shakespeare, Charles Darwin: Dennis Hamley
Tutankhamun: Martin Oliver
Joan of Arc: Victoria Parker

ISBN 978-1-84810-308-5

Printed in China

British Library Cataloguing-in-Publication Data
A catalogue record for this book is available from the British Library

Made with paper from a sustainable forest

www.mileskelly.net   info@mileskelly.net

CONTENTS

Tutankhamun

1 **DIGGING UP THE PAST** 9
2 **A NEW PHARAOH** 13
3 **THE PHARAOH'S PYRAMID OF POWER** 22
4 **THE GODS SQUAD** 41
5 **MIGHTY PYRAMIDS** 51
6 **MUMMY-MAKING MASTERCLASS** 62
7 **LIFTING THE LID ON TUTANKHAMUN'S COFFIN** 66
8 **EGYPT-MANIA** 75

Julius Caesar

1 FAMILY ALBUM 81
2 BABY IN DANGER 91
3 ADULT LIFE STARTS WITH A TOGA 102
4 DISASTERS FOR CAESAR 111
5 HARD LESSONS 119
6 ROME IN TURMOIL 128
7 WHAT NEXT? 138
8 GAUL 151
9 CIVIL WAR OR WORLD WAR? 158
10 THE FATAL MISTAKE 164
11 FRIENDS, ROMANS, COUNTRYMEN... 167

Joan of Arc

1 Go Get 'em, Girls   171
2 Rowing Royals and Suffering Citizens   176
3 The God Squad   188
4 Tried and Tested   202
5 Arise, Sir Joan!   212
6 Joan's Predictions Come True…
    Well, Some of Them, Anyway!   227
7 A Dirty Dungeon and a Dismal Death   244
8 Sorry! We Made a Mistake   254

Napoleon

1 Boney'll Get You!   261
2 The Rich Get Rich and the Poor Get Nothing   270
3 The King Must Die   279
4 A Gentlemanly Occupation   288
5 Brilliant Soldier – Brilliant Organiser   296
6 Kill Napoleon   311
7 The End of the Empire   320

Charles Darwin

1 What did people think before Darwin?   333
2 Who made Charles Darwin?   342
3 A lab in the shed   346
4 Tiny details, big questions   351
5 A professor, a brown owl, a beetle and a girlfriend   357

6 Sailing on the *Beagle*   364
7 Right around the world – part 1   370
8 Right around the world – part 2   380
9 The new life and marriage   389
10 Life at Down House   397
11 *The Origin of Species*   404
12 And afterwards?   411
13 Where shall we bury Charles?   416
14 And now?   418

William Shakespeare

1 He Makes Me Sick   423
2 Is This How It Was?   429
3 What Happened Next?   434
4 The Big World Outside   443
5 Plagues, Plays and Puritans   449
6 Poems, Patrons and more Plague   456
7 Some Answers   461
8 Shakespeare in Love – sort of...   465
9 Into the Globe   470
10 "Sad stories about the death of kings."   474
11 Any more Questions?   484
12 Feeling Rotten   486
13 Goodbye Elizabeth – Hello James   493
14 William's Last Years in London   497
15 The End   502
16 So What Have We Got?   507

ABOUT THE AUTHORS   510

Tutankhamun
and other Mummy's boys

Chapter 1

DIGGING UP THE PAST

History lessons are full of kings and queens, aren't they? And all of them dust off the same old mouldy facts about when they lived, who they married and when they died. If only there was some juicy gossip and riveting revelations about them. After all, who wouldn't want to be a king or queen? Surely it must have been great fun to be a member of royalty and enjoy red carpet treatment wherever they went.

Or was it? What was royal life really like? Learn how Tutankhamun and the other pharaohs of ancient Egypt actually lived. Discover the good bits, the bad bits and the downright ugly bits. You'll find out how Tutankhamun came to the throne, how he spent his days, and you'll even have the chance to get under his skin – literally – as we investigate a suspected case of Mummy murder.

While Tutankhamun and the pharaohs are the stars of the ancient world, we wouldn't know about their lives if it wasn't for the hard work of historians and archaeologists. Films with characters like Indiana Jones make archaeology look incredibly exciting, but the reality is often very different. Most archaeologists spend many frustrating and difficult years working with small clues but just occasionally, years of study and hard work can pay off spectacularly. Nowhere was this more the case than during one hot dusty day in 1922.

Howard Carter was an archaeologist who had been working in the Valley of the Kings for many years. He had already discovered several tombs but all of them had been robbed and were almost empty. However, Carter wasn't going to give up. Years before, a small cup had been found with the name Tutankhamun on it and Carter was sure that the tomb of this little-known pharaoh was somewhere in the valley.

His sponsor, Lord Carnarvon, was not an impatient man but even his deep pockets were beginning to reach their limit. Excavating was an expensive business and he had very little to show for his work so far. Carter knew that he was on the verge of running out of funds and was working feverishly...

"Mr Carter, Mr Carter!"

The archaeologist straightened up to trace the source of the call. He saw a crowd of workers running towards him in a cloud of dust.

"What is it?" he asked above the babble of excited voices. "Just one at a time. Talk slowly."

His Arabic was not fluent but there was no mistaking the urgency and sign language from the men. He followed them out of the camp and down into the valley. There, in the rocky rubble, they stopped and pointed – to a step.

Carter's heart leapt and he ordered his workers to clear away the rubble. Grabbing a shovel, he joined in and helped them as they uncovered more steps leading to a blocked doorway. With his heart pounding, Carter made a hole in the doorway. Then he noticed something very special on the plaster and stopped. He raced back to his camp and sent a telegram to Lord Carnarvon saying,

> # TELEGRAM:
> ## HAVE MADE A WONDERFUL DISCOVERY STOP A MAGNIFICENT TOMB WITH SEALS INTACT STOP

Carter ordered the tomb to be resealed and posted armed guards beside it. He waited in a fever of excitement and anticipation for Carnarvon's visit. It took almost three weeks for him to make the journey but finally he arrived.

The steps to the tomb were cleared once again and the duo made their way down into the gloom. Aware that nobody had walked this way for millennia, they came to a passageway leading to a door. Carter made a hole into the doorway and held a torch up to the gap.

"Well," hissed Lord Carnarvon. "Can you see anything?"

At last, Carter's eyes grew used to the darkness beyond and his voice trembled as he replied, "Yes, wonderful things."

What they were about to find wasn't just Tutankhamun's final resting place, but a time machine. The journey that the duo had started would take them back over 3000 years to a time when an extraordinary civilization flourished, a time when the pharaohs ruled with absolute power.

Chapter 2

A NEW PHARAOH

The dawn sun rose over the horizon, its golden rays glittered on the magnificent River Nile and lit up the bustling brick-built city of Thebes. Despite the early hour, a large crowd had already left the city and made their way to the magnificent Great Temple of Ammun in nearby Karnak. It was the start of the new year and one of the most important days for a long time – the coronation of the new pharaoh, Tutankhamun.

The dawn air was heavy with the smell of incense. For many days, priests had been busy sacrificing animals on temple altars and performing other ancient rituals. After a period of great unrest, the court had returned to its traditional capital of Thebes and the temples had been opened again. A great sense of optimism ran through the assembled crowd who hoped that this time would signal a period of peace and wealth. Perhaps the new pharaoh, Tutankhamun, would live to a ripe old age and rule over his people wisely.

The prince has already entered a shrine where the blue war crown has been placed on his head. Then he steps out and the high priests place all the crowns of Egypt, one after the other, on his head. The symbols of power, the golden crook and staff, are placed in his hands. At last, he is now the new pharaoh.

A hush and an expectant gasp ripples along the huge crowd as the temple gates are thrown open, giving them their first view of their new ruler. Ordinary people, rich courtiers, even the vizier, all bow down before the figure in front of them. Clad in brilliant, brightly coloured clothes and with the sun glinting off a glittering array of golden jewellery, Tutankhamun appears before his subjects.

The spectators at the back of the crowd crane their necks and narrow their eyes to get a better look at their new ruler. "Is that him?" whispered one. "He's very small." "Of course," came the reply. "But he is nine years old!"

14

Long live the King

We are delighted to announce the 100th birthday of our glorious pharaoh. A celebration feast will be held at the palace and priests are giving thanks for our beloved ruler at temples throughout the kingdom.

Few people can now remember King Pepy II coming to the throne at the age of nine years but we're delighted to add our best wishes to the longest-reigning pharaoh in the history of Egypt and hope that his rule continues for many years to come.

ROYAL REVELATIONS

That's right, at an age when the nearest that most people come to ruling is in maths lessons, Tutankhamun, like Pepy before him, became pharaoh of Egypt. And if you're surprised at how young the boy king was when he was crowned, you'd better sit down now. Royal families always seem to produce their fair share of amazing facts and royal revelations – and the pharaohs were no exception. If they had newspapers, this is what they'd say...

THE EGYPTIAN TIMES

Royal Scoop - new King is a Queen.

It's official and you heard it here first - our new king is a queen. A spokesperson for the palace has confirmed that our new ruler is Queen Hatshepsut.

"As the most powerful person in the kingdom," said the spokesperson, "Queen Hatshepsut has decided to bow to the wishes of the people and become pharaoh." Despite this break with royal tradition, our new pharaoh is determined to keep up with some well-established customs.

"As all pharaohs are the sons of the god Re, I can confirm that I will wear men's clothes and the ceremonial beard of power. I shall also ensure that whenever my image appears, I shall be painted in male form."

However, rumours have reached us that many people are not happy with our king being a queen. A group of powerful courtiers have made it plain they would prefer a more traditional ruler but will give Hatshepsut a chance.

The Times thinks...
Here at the Egyptian Times, we predict a successful reign for the Queen but don't think that the trend for queenly kings will catch on!

Pharaoh Marries - Again!

Sister weds brother

Love is in the air and wedding bells are once again ringing out over the royal palace as King Sneferu announces he is getting married - for the 20th time. Our marriage correspondent has confirmed that invitations have been sent throughout the kingdom and that the king has decided against a wedding list saying, "I think we've got everything by now."

Breaking news just in:

The pharaoh and his favourite wife have just announced a double celebration. In order to keep the royal bloodline pure, their eldest son and daughter will also marry each other.

Minding your P's and K's

The third of a series of tips on correct behaviour by our court etiquette expert:

We have already covered replying to a royal invitation and what to wear — now it is time to deal with addressing the pharaoh. This is a most important subject as calling him by the wrong name can literally mean the difference between life and death.

Calling our ruler 'King' is not only wrong but could be considered an insult that may be punished by the death penalty. Never forget that he is much more than a king, he is a god directly descended from the sun-god, Re.

The correct term that should always be used is 'Pharaoh'. This means 'palace' and refers to the fact that the pharaoh's body is the earthly house or palace of Re.

DISHING THE DIRT ON DYNASTIES

Tutankhamun's coronation in 1333BC came at around the halfway point in the rule of the pharaohs. One of the most incredible things about the pharaohs is that they were kings of Egypt for so long – around 3000 years. In fact, they ruled for such an amazingly long time that the pyramids, temples and other remains they left behind were considered old even by the ancient Greeks and Romans.

Of course, throughout the thousands of years that the pharaohs were in power, there were hundreds of different rulers. The first true pharaoh was a king called Menes. When he came to power, Egypt was split into two different kingdoms. Menes was king of Upper Egypt and in around 3200BC, he conquered Lower Egypt. By joining the two different territories, he created the country known as ancient Egypt.

In addition to this, Menes also founded the first Egyptian dynasty (posh word used to describe a succession of rulers from the same family). It's very difficult to work out the exact dates that individual pharaohs ruled and historians would have been in a fix if it hadn't been for a priest called Manetho.

Did you know? Manetho was the first Ancient Egypt historian. He had the bright idea of writing the first history of Egypt in around 300BC. He recorded the name of each pharaoh then grouped each of them into 30 different dynasties – a system still used by modern day Egyptian experts.

THE PHARAOH FAMILY TREE

Thanks to Manetho's hard work, historians have been able to trace Tutankhamun's family tree. The boy king ruled during a period known as the New Kingdom. His predecessors were four kings all called Amenophis but his father, Amenophis IV, changed his name to Akhenaten when he was crowned.

Akhenaten ruled for seventeen years with his principal queen, Nefertiti, but Tutankhamun's mother was another of the pharaoh's wives, called Kiya. After his father died, Egypt was ruled by a mysterious king, called Ankhkhprerue Smenkhkaredjerkhepru until Tutankhamun came to the throne. When he was king, Tutankhamun married his half sister, Ankhesenamun.

When Tutankhamun died, there was a danger that the dynasty would die out but it was saved when Tutankhamun's great uncle Ay became pharaoh. However, the only way he could do this was by marrying Tutankhamun's widow, Ankhesenamun – who was his own granddaughter!

Chapter 3

THE PHARAOH'S
PYRAMID OF POWER

Marrying your own granddaughter might seem like an extraordinary thing to do but then pharaohs were fairly extraordinary. The ancient Egyptians believed in a strict social order in which everyone knew their place. Reaching the position of pharaoh was a bit like climbing to the top of a pyramid. Once you were at the summit, you literally had the world at your feet.

Pharaoh

STATUS:

son of Re, the sun-god, you are a god in human form. You are the all-powerful ruler of the country and as such you are kept away from your subjects, surrounded by nobles and other influential advisers.

DISTINGUISHING FEATURES:

easily recognised by the symbols he (or she) carries, including bull's tail, beard, crook and staff.

OTHER TITLES:

Chief Priest and Commander of the Armies

JOB DESCRIPTION:

to lead the country, rule the law courts, head the army and decide trade issues.

QUALIFICATIONS AND TRAINING:

more of a question of being born in the right family at the right time. However, if you are particularly ruthless, you could become pharaoh by force.

vizier

PROFILE

Vizier

STATUS:

second most powerful person in the kingdom.

OTHER TITLES:

Chief Judge.

JOB DESCRIPTION:

to ensure the smooth running of the country. You keep your eye on every department in the government and are in charge of the law courts.

QUALIFICATIONS AND TRAINING:

usually a member of the royal (or a noble) family. Hardworking and hopefully honest. If ambitious, you could be tempted to depose the pharaoh.

minister

Ministers and 'King's Friends'

STATUS:

just below the vizier in terms of importance.

JOB TITLES:

ministers have different titles such as Director of Building Works, Keeper of the Crown Jewels and Controller of the State Granaries. Favoured courtiers are friends of the king and have other job titles such as Royal Sandal Carrier and Keeper of the King's Clothes.

JOB DESCRIPTION:

fairly obvious, depending on the job title. However, the Keeper of the Secret of all Royal Sayings isn't a translator but decides who gets to talk to the pharaoh.

QUALIFICATIONS AND TRAINING:

once again, it is more a case of who you know than what you know with the best jobs being snaffled by the friends and family of the pharaoh.

Nomarch

Nomarchs

STATUS:

nomarchs have little influence in court but are in charge of their own small territories within the kingdom.

JOB DESCRIPTION:

to control their local areas. Must obey the pharaoh's orders and be prepared to raise an army if the kingdom is attacked.

QUALIFICATIONS AND TRAINING:

once again, being born in the right family is the most important attribute but influence can be gained through force.

Scribe

PROFILE

Scribes

STATUS:

varied. Status ranges from lowly local letter writer to ministry scribe to Superintendent of Documents at court.

JOB DESCRIPTION:

to learn how to write hieroglyphics and keep written records. Generally it is better not to come up with ideas yourself but to suggest that your best ideas have come from your superior. Accuracy is not vital but keeping your employer happy is. Historical records should always reveal the pharaoh as a great ruler and strong commander.

QUALIFICATIONS AND TRAINING:

extreme dedication required. Scribe school is very hard work and children are regularly beaten (so maybe your teachers aren't so bad after all). A strong stomach is required for army scribes, as the most common way to check enemy casualties is by cutting off and counting the right hands of dead soldiers.

Priest

Priests

STATUS:

rises depending on your position within a temple and the popularity of your god.

JOB DESCRIPTION:

there are many tasks within the temples. You may begin by running the temple's workshops and estates before serving the gods direct. Only a favoured few are allowed into the temple that houses the spirit or 'ka' of your god. Followers will leave food and drink for you to give to the god's ka, keeping it alive in the world beyond the grave.

QUALIFICATION AND TRAINING:

many years devoted to one god would normally see you rise through the ranks. Your ultimate goal would be to become high priest.

Craftsman

PROFILE

Craftsmen

STATUS:

> generally high if your skills are appreciated by
> wealthy customers, although all villages have
> their own craftsmen making everyday essentials.
> In general, your ability will determine your status.

JOB DESCRIPTION:

> extremely varied, depending on your craft.
> Craftsmen include potters and basket makers
> working for ordinary people. However, special
> villages are constructed for craftsmen such as
> painters, sculptors, jewellery makers, stone
> masons and goldsmiths who are employed by
> the pharaoh.

QUALIFICATION AND TRAINING:

> training is often given by being apprenticed to a
> certain master craftsman and learning is done on
> the job.

Soldier

PROFILE

Soldiers

STATUS:

depends on when you join up. Until 1600BC
(or thereabouts), the Egyptian army was poorly
equipped with heavy shields, small axes and fairly
useless bows. However, after being defeated by
invaders from neighbouring Hyksos, a
professional army was formed and the status of
soldiers rose.

JOB DESCRIPTION:

varies depending on whether you serve in the
infantry, as a bowman or charioteer. However,
battles are always fought according to strict rules.
An agreed time and place is set when armies fight
each other in daylight on open ground.

QUALIFICATIONS AND TRAINING:

training is given in barracks, then soldiers can
return home unless needed to fight or work for
the pharaoh.

Peasant

Peasants

STATUS:

lowly.

JOB DESCRIPTION:

to feed yourself and your family, to provide the
workforce for the kingdom.

QUALIFICATIONS AND TRAINING:

at this low level, you'll probably learn your skills
on the job. Most peasants are farmers who plant
wheat and barley and keep birds and a few cattle.
Although work is hard, peasants are free men as
the only slaves in the kingdom are prisoners of
war or convicts.

ALL THE FUN OF THE PHARAOH

So, what would life have been like for Tutankhamun? Being the all-powerful ruler of the country sounds like phantastic phun, but did the boy king have a right royal time or a right rotten time of it? Find out by reading our unofficial diary.

MID-MORNING

I am beginning to settle into my new bedroom in the Palace. I had a good night's sleep followed by a great breakfast and I was really looking forward to the day ahead until Uncle Ay appeared. He said that a delegation from Nubia, one of our conquered countries, has arrived in Thebes to pay tribute to me.

I asked Uncle Ay what I should do and he said that we would have to hold a banquet this evening to accept their tributes. He said that he would organise everything and I shouldn't worry. After he had gone, I began to feel a bit hungry. I ordered a snack of my favourite date sweets then I thought I could play a game with my new wife, Ankhesenamun.

I feel a bit cross with Ankhesenamun. She laughed when she saw me playing with a spinning top and didn't want to play catch so I said she could choose the game she wanted to play. Unfortunately, she loves sennet and so we played that.

Well, all I can say is that Ankhesenamun had all the luck of the dice. I hate that game! Anyway, she was about to beat me when Uncle Ay reappeared and told me that our boat was ready for our hunting. I stopped playing straightaway and told Ankhesenamun that we would play sennet again sometime — but not for ages.

cheat!

my drawing – T

LUNCH

...was delicious. My new Chief Steward is
doing a good job. The cooking staff have
finally got the message that I hate lamb and
they brought my favourite joint of goat
instead. Uncle Ay joined us for lunch, saying
that his favourite was bread mixed with nuts
and spices. After my goat, I polished off a
plate of melons and washed it down with
some wine.

AFTERNOON

I think that I might have overdone it at
lunch. I can't remember anything about our
trip to the river. Perhaps the wine wasn't
such a good idea.

Still, there was plenty of time to look
around as we were rowed towards the
marshy hunting area. The Nile was really
busy. I saw simple papyrus boats and large
wooden vessels, piled high with timber.
Along the way, we disturbed some birds

from the reeds and we all practised bringing them down with throwsticks. I'm not sure if I hit any of them but my courtiers all said that I was a great hunter — and I smiled in agreement.

grrrrrr!

Then, at last we spotted our prey — a hippopotamus. It was huge and had the biggest teeth I've ever seen. The beast struggled but eventually our spears found their target. Even when it was wounded, the animal still tried to struggle and almost tipped our boat over. I saw crocodiles swimming towards us and they certainly dined well on the hippopotamus that afternoon. We were all happy at our hunting success and sang all the way back to the palace.

I was feeling very tired after hunting and I really wanted to go to bed but Uncle Ay reminded me of the banquet I had ordered.

I had a good long splash in the bath then my staff dressed me in fresh, clean garments and my symbols of power — what I really hate the most is the ceremonial beard, it always scratches my chin!

Just then Ankhesenamun came in and massaged oils and perfumes over my neck and shoulders. My wife had really made an effort and was looking a picture in her finest linen clothes. The beautiful gold necklace that I had given her was glittering in the light of the setting sun. To finish off the whole stunning effect, she had put colours all around her eyes, and she was wearing a fresh wig covered with scented beeswax.

The banquet was held in the great hall of the palace and was a great success. My craftsmen have worked really hard over the last few weeks and the gold inlays and bright paints glistened throughout the building. Uncle Ay suggested that I should reward my Steward with a gold necklace — which seems like a good idea.

I could tell that the Nubian ambassadors were impressed when they saw me. I couldn't wait to see what presents they'd brought and I was delighted to receive their gold, ivory and leopard skins.

Best of all, was the latest addition to my menagerie. We already have baboons and an elephant but this new arrival is my favourite. It's huge — taller than three men standing on each other's shoulders — and it has a magnificent neck. When I asked a bit more about the animal, I was told that it eats mainly grass and that it is called a giraffe.

Oh dear, it really is very late — way past my bedtime. Uncle Ay made sure I didn't nod off in front of the guests which is just as well as I was feeling very tired. He mentioned that my ministers would like to talk to me. The Overseer of the Treasury and the Head of Irrigation have urgent matters they wish to discuss. To be honest, I don't really understand most of the things they talk about so I think I shall let Uncle Ay take care of them instead. Anyway, I have my own plans for tomorrow. Uncle Ay has suggested that I look into the building of some temples and consider a tomb but I'd much rather go and feed the giraffe.

OFFICIAL DUTIES

Of course, there was a bit more to being pharaoh than just hunting and feasting. Nowadays, royal families tend to stick to things like opening supermarkets, bridges and sporting events but which of the following official duties do you think Tutankhamun would have been expected to carry out?

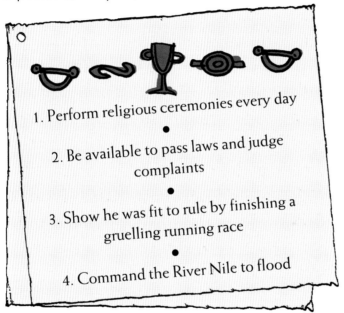

1. Perform religious ceremonies every day

•

2. Be available to pass laws and judge complaints

•

3. Show he was fit to rule by finishing a gruelling running race

•

4. Command the River Nile to flood

Answer: *All of them.*

However, if Tutankhamun was worried about overdoing it, we can reveal how a Pharaoh could make light work of his duties.

1. You must make offerings to your fellow gods on a daily basis or the sun won't rise and the world will end. If you're not in the mood or would like a lie-in, the solution is quite simple – just pull rank and ask your priests to do it for you.

2. As leader of the country, you rule the law courts. You are the only person able to pass the death sentence and in theory, all your subjects have the right to appeal personally to you for justice. Once again, a few simple steps will help ease the burden. Firstly, give your vizier responsibility for the courts then ensure your officials keep the public out of hearing distance. If this fails, you could always pretend to be deaf.

3. This is a tough one to avoid but there's no need to worry about fitness training too soon. The running event which marks the end of Heb-seb Festival only takes place once you have been in power for thirty years.

4. This is one duty that you can't really avoid but then this ceremony only takes place once a year. You are expected to demonstrate your god-like power by starting the flooding of the River Nile to your grateful subjects. This event is vital to the health of your country as the flood waters cover the desert, giving it a top layer of soil and turning it into fertile land for farming. The Nile regularly begins to flood on the 15th July but unfortunately the amount of flooding is sometimes unpredictable – still, even pharaohs can have an off day.

goats-milk shake.. fries and cheeseburger...

Chapter 4

THE GODS SQUAD

Tutankhamun wouldn't have had to bother about ordinary things like having enough food and money to go around but there was one thing that even the pharaoh worried about – keeping the gods happy.

In ancient Egypt, there were lots of different gods who controlled the world and everything that happened in it (a bit like your head teacher, really – only this lot could be even crueller). Priests taught the Egyptian people that anyone who failed to pay their due respects to the gods was in big trouble. If you offended the gods they would not only make your life miserable – they would also turn your afterlife into a not-so-living nightmare.

When your turn came to die, you would face three of the greatest gods in the Hall of Two Truths. The gods would place your heart on one side of a set of scales and place a feather on the other. However, as you might imagine, this was no ordinary feather but was a feather that held all the lies of your life. If your heart outweighed the feather then you would enter Yaru (the Egyptian Afterlife) but if you failed, your heart was thrown to ferocious Devourer and you would be condemned to spend the rest of your afterlife with the souls of other evil, wicked people.

PREMIER LEAGUE GODS

Making sure the gods were happy with you was an expensive and time-consuming business. Keeping up with all of them wouldn't have left you with much time for anything else, so most people chose to worship a few individual gods. As a premier league person, Tutankhamun was probably only interested in keeping the premier league gods on his side. He knew he had to play his cards right.

OSIRIS, THE GOD OF LIFE AND DEATH, RULER OF THE UNDERWORLD
Special duties: teaching people to farm the soil.

ISIS, WIFE OF OSIRIS
Special duties: protecting women
and children.

HORUS
Distinguishing features:
falcon head.
Special duties: looking after
the pharaoh.

RE, THE SUN GOD
Distinguishing features: sun
head-dress and beard.
 Special duties: as the national
 god of Egypt, Re is
 responsible for keeping the
 nation safe and prosperous.

THOTH, THE GOD OF WISDOM
Distinguishing features:
ibis head.
Special duties: invents
speech and hieroglyphics.

ANUBIS, THE GOD OF THE DEAD
Distinguishing features:
jackal head.
Special duties: decides on
your fate during the afterlife.

SEKHMET, THE GODDESS OF WAR
Distinguishing features:
lion's head.
Special duties: ensuring
success in battles.

SOBEK, THE GOD OF WATER
Distinguishing features:
crocodile head.
Special duties: responsible
for water supplies to the
kingdom.

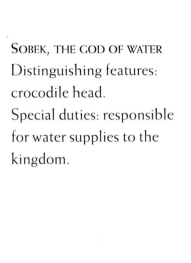

BAST, GODDESS OF JOY, MUSIC
AND DANCING
Distinguishing features: a cat.
Special duties: responsible
for fun.

SECOND DIVISION DEMI-GODS

If you were lower down the social scale, your daily concerns would be different to the pharaoh's and so would your favourite gods. In the case of these demi-gods, appearances could often be deceptive and some of the strangest-looking ones were thought to be friendly.

 Twarat was a huge, pregnant hippopotamus whose appearance was frightening enough to scare away any misfortune during childbirth.

 Despite looking like a cobra, Renenutet would help during the harvest.

Of all these demi-gods, Bes was probably the most popular. Despite being a bandy-legged dwarf with the ears, whiskers and tail of a lion, he was believed to protect all members of the family and to keep everyone happy.

WORRY LIKE AN EGYPTIAN

With so many gods in charge of so many different aspects of life, it was no surprise that all Egyptians were superstitious. From the pharaoh right down to farm labourer, all ancient Egyptians believed that dreams could predict what would happen in the future. What do you think each of the following dreams meant?

Interpreting Dreams

1. You dream that your teeth are falling out.
A. You need to see a dentist.
B. Someone close to you is going to die.
C. Someone close to you is going to give you money.

2. Someone gives you white bread in your dream.
A. This means you are going to be lucky.
B. This means you are going to be unlucky.
C. This means you are hungry.

3. You have the face of a leopard.
A. This is a good dream, meaning you will become an important leader.
B. This is a bad dream, meaning you will soon become ill.
C. This is a bad dream, meaning Egypt will be attacked.

Answers: 1B, 2A, 3A.

As if worrying about dreams wasn't enough, the Egyptians also believed that whole days were unlucky. One of the most dangerous days of the year, worse even than a distant relative's wedding or a French test, was the day of Sekhmet – the goddess who sent diseases.

On unlucky days many people simply stayed indoors to avoid bad luck. Another way to protect yourself was to wear lucky charms or amulets while your friendly neighbourhood priests also offered a solution to bad dreams or other worries – simply place offerings at the appropriate temple. Of course, it was just coincidence that this would also help the priests become richer and more powerful.

DR DO-ALOT

If all your precautions failed and you became ill, you were in with a good chance of getting better. Ancient Egyptian doctors were extraordinarily well-trained and well-equipped. The royal family employed their own specialist physicians for eye problems, stomach disorders – even surgery – while ordinary people could visit doctors at The House of Life, a sort of surgery that was attached to temples.

Many of the remedies prescribed by Egyptian doctors were extraordinarily effective.

From: The House of Life Surgery, Thebes.

Ailment: infected wound.

Treatment: wrap in leaves containing aspirin to help treat pain then powder with copper and sodium salts to dry it out.

Ailment: broken bone
Treatment: set broken bone with cast made from cream and flour. Prescribe rest until healing process is complete.

Ailment: parasitic worm
Treatment: make cut in affected area. Wind stick around worm to remove it then treat with salts to dry the wound. Stitch incision then bind with bandages.

Ailment: weakness
Treatment: make up herbal brew of beer, cow's milk and castor oil to build up patient's strength.

However, not all prescriptions were quite so good and some were more a case of kill or cure. Here's one remedy that most people would find hard to swallow.

Ailment: severe cough
Treatment: take one dead mouse and swallow whole.

Chapter 5

MIGHTY PYRAMIDS

Of course, there was one thing that amulets, prayers and even the best doctors couldn't prevent – death. However, Tutankhamun's predecessors often seemed to have been less worried about dying than making sure they went out in style. Many of them would have made great boy scouts as they lived by the motto 'be prepared'. During their reigns, they spent huge amounts of time (not to mention money) planning and constructing some of the most magnificent tombs ever built – the mighty majestic pyramids.

Everyone has seen photos of the pyramids, someone you know may even have visited them, but how much do you actually know about them? Turn yourself into an expert with our fantastic fact attack.

DID YOU KNOW?

1. A total of 96 pyramids have been discovered in Egypt. They were all built between 2700 and 1640BC.

2. The pyramids were constructed to contain and protect the body of dead pharaohs. Without the body, the pharaoh's spirit could not survive but if it was kept safe, the Egyptians believed the power of their ruler would help preserve the kingdom.

3. Three different styles of pyramid were built. The earliest pyramids had flat-topped layers, all built on top of each other. The pyramid built for King Sneferu is a one-off, known as the bent pyramid, while the most common style is called the straight-sided pyramid.

4. All pyramids were constructed on the west bank of the Nile for religious reasons. They were also built on solid rock bases above the flood level for practical reasons.

5. The Great Pyramid of Cheops is the oldest stone-built structure in the world. Its base covers an area the size of eight football pitches.

THE MIGHTY MYSTERIOUS PYRAMIDS

So far, so straightforward – but the more people investigated the mighty pyramids, the more they realised they could be renamed the mighty mysterious pyramids. Despite years of study and hard work from archaeologists and scientists, the pyramids seem to have raised more questions than they have answered. Read on as we lift the lid of the unsolved secrets of the pyramids.

WHY WAS THE PYRAMID SHAPE CHOSEN BY THE PHARAOHS?

Many ingenious explanations have been put forward to answer this question. Some experts think that the pyramids acted like a staircase for the dead pharaoh to walk up and meet the sun-god. Other historians have suggested that the shape shows the first part of the earth that rose above waters during creation according to Egyptian myths. Another group has suggested that the pyramid shape was chosen purely for practical reasons – it was strong and long-lasting.

HOW WERE THE PYRAMIDS BUILT?

Once again, nobody really knows. You've probably seen pictures of people dragging huge blocks up ramps of sand and this may well be how the pyramids were constructed – but no one can prove that this method was definitely used. However, one theory that slaves were used to make the pyramids has been disproved by historians. Records have been discovered showing that skilled pyramid workers were paid partly in garlic and radishes.

THE MYSTERY OF THE GREAT PYRAMID OF CHEOPS

The greatest pyramid of them all is also the most mysterious. Built by King Cheops, it had stood undisturbed for over three thousand years before another mighty leader, the Caliph of Baghdad, decided to try and enter it. With a little help from a huge army of men, he tunnelled his way through its huge stone blocks. At the centre of the pyramids, he eventually discovered a chamber for Cheops' queen and the king's burial chamber. Inside this huge room was a large coffin. Surrounded by his men, the Caliph watched as the coffin was opened. He ordered his men back and stared at... nothing. The coffin was empty! Nobody else had ever broken into the pyramid, so what had happened to the body of the pharaoh? Again, there are many suggestions but no one has come up with the final answer.

A MOST MYSTERIOUS ENCOUNTER

When the Emperor Napoleon visited the same pyramid at the end of the eighteenth century, he also had a most mysterious encounter. After spending some time alone in the king's burial chamber, he reappeared pale and shaking. Later in his life, he mentioned the visit and hinted that he had seen something

amazing. When he was dying he seemed to be on the verge of revealing his secret only to stop himself saying that no one would believe him. Shortly afterwards, he died, taking the mystery of his encounter with him.

 ## THE MYSTERIOUS PRESERVING POWER OF THE PYRAMIDS

Many people have noticed the mysterious preserving powers of pyramids. Food seems to stay fresh longer if placed within them and in the 1960s an engineer even sold his patented design of plastic model pyramids as razor blade sharpeners. Once again, nobody seems able to explain these powers.

SPOT THE DIFFERENCE

If the pyramids looked spectacular from the outside, their interiors were just as impressive. In most of the tombs, the pharaoh's burial chamber was large and the whole tomb would be richly painted with pictures and hieroglyphics showing the magnificent deeds performed by the pharaoh during his life.

However, when Tutankhuman's tomb was opened, it consisted only of a short corridor and four small rooms: the antechamber, the annexe, the burial chamber and the treasury. Even more surprising was the fact that the walls of the burial chamber showed no scenes from the boy king's life – just his funeral and meetings with gods in the afterlife.

After plenty of head scratching, archaeologists think they may have come up with the answer, but what do you think it is?

another Fire-exit Cartouche

Archaeologists think that Tutankhamun died before his official tomb could be completed and, as a result, his body was buried in a smaller, private tomb.

The differences between Tutankhamun's tomb and the pyramids don't end there. The pyramids had one large drawback – they acted as a magnet for tomb robbers. It was all very well building a huge tomb and cramming it full of treasures but it was another matter to try and keep it safe.

Tutankhamun's ancestors came up with some ingenious ways to try and stop tomb robbers. Which of the following do you think were used?

1. Building false doors.

2. Killing servants who worked on the tomb.

3. Using huge boulders to block passages.

4. Concealing trapdoors.

   Answer: all of them except 2

1. Tomb designers and architects didn't just try building false doors to mislead tomb robbers, they even tried fake corridors and false stairs that lead nowhere.

2. When some of the earliest pharaohs died, their servants were also killed so they could accompany and serve their masters in the afterlife. (This bloodthirsty practice was soon stopped and models were included in the tomb instead.) There is no evidence that tomb builders and architects were also killed to prevent them stealing from the tomb but if any robbers were caught then they would be put to death.

3. Having placed the pharaoh's body and treasures in the tomb, huge rocks and boulders were used to block tunnels and passageways leading to the burial chamber.

4. In an attempt to fool robbers, enormous blocks were placed in front of tomb entrances and plastered over. When robbers uncovered the plaster they would find the block and think it was part of the tomb wall – they wouldn't notice the way into the tomb by the hidden trapdoor above.

PLAN B

The most important difference between Tutankhamun's tomb and his fellow pharaohs' burial places is that his was the only one to survive intact. When all of their best efforts to stop tomb robbing failed, the pharaohs and their courtiers switched to plan B – moving their tombs and hiding them. The place they chose was a narrow valley in a desolate area called The Valley of the Kings. Most of Tutankhamun's predecessors were buried here in tombs cut into the solid rock but even this desperate move only managed to save Tutankhamun's tomb – the rest were all robbed.

It's not hard to understand why tomb robbers thought it was worthwhile risking their lives to steal from the pharaoh's tombs, but you might wonder why the pharaohs insisted on being buried with so many rich, valuable items. However, it wasn't a case of showing off, it was all due to religious beliefs.

Like all pharaohs, Tutankhamun believed that the night after his burial, he would make a journey by boat into the Underworld. The nocturnal trip would lead to him being reborn at dawn with the gods and to ensure he didn't get lost on the route, he could even bring a 'Book of the Dead', a sort of Egyptian A–Z of how to get there safely.

Having arrived, the pharaoh could then begin his life in the spirit world and, as a result, his tomb should contain everything he would want in the afterlife. Some of the items buried with Tutankhamun

would be exactly what you'd
expect to find:

A throne

Chariots

Hunting statue

Folding bed

His tomb also included
some things you might
not expect to find:

Model boats

Gilded wooden sled

Writing implements

365 wooden figures
of workmen – to work for
him during the afterlife

Along with some
things you wouldn't
WANT to find:

Two mummified babies

Four jars containing the
pharaoh's internal organs.

Other pharaohs took different things with them.

Chapter 6

Welcome to mummy making masterclass.

MUMMY MAKING
MASTERCLASS

Of course, all these preparations would have been wasted without the one vital ingredient – the body of the pharaoh. As you might imagine, this wasn't just a simple case of putting the dead body into the tomb. The Egyptians believed that the body had to be preserved so the person's spirit could survive in the afterlife. As a result, embalming became a real skill.

WELCOME TO THE MUMMY MAKING MASTERCLASS

The secret to a really professional longer-lasting job is preparation. You will need the following:

1. Premises

It's a good idea to site your business in a tent. This is cooler and lets the breeze waft away the smell of decaying flesh although sweet-smelling perfumes and oils can help too.

Call your tent, the 'Beautiful House' – an example of ancient Egyptian humour.

2. Tools

You'll need an array of tools including sharp knives, chisels and iron hooks. Don't forget a state-of-the-art embalming table with a slatted wooden top for easy access to all parts of the body.

3. Workforce

In addition to a strong stomach, a thick skin is required. The people who cut up the pharaoh's body are often cursed for injuring him. Keep a look out for potential new recruits as business expands. In the early days, only rich nobles and pharaohs could afford to be mummified but over time, more and more people are being embalmed.

4. Other essentials

Natron – you'll find this salty chemical for embalming around the shores of lakes near Cairo.

Bandages – made of linen, you'll need hundreds of metres of bandages for wrapping bodies.

Canopic jars – small jars that are used to contain the internal organs of the bodies. The jars are sealed with specially carved stoppers, representing four gods who will protect your insides. *Hapy* is an ape-headed god who looks after the lungs, *Duamutef*, a jackal-headed god, who looks after the stomach, *Qebehsanuef* keeps a hawk's eye on your intestines while *Imsety* guards the liver.

You probably can't wait to start but before you begin slicing and dicing, pay attention to our top tip of the day – **MAKE SURE YOU RECEIVE PAYMENT IN ADVANCE!**

Well done. Now you're properly prepared it's time to follow our simple steps to making a perfect mummy.

Step 1   Take body of dead pharaoh and transport it to your Beautiful House.

Step 2   Once the body has been undressed, place it on the embalming table and begin by removing the brain (this is usually done by chiselling up through the nose then using a hook to pull out the brain). Then clean the mouth and fill with sweet-smelling oils.

Step 3 Now pack the empty skull with the embalming chemical natron. Add powder to fill the space.

Step 4 It's time for the 'ripper-up embalmer' to do his job. Allow him to cut open the stomach and remove its contents. These are cleaned and washed. Then fill the hole with spices and sew up the body again.

Step 5 Remove all other organs – but leave the heart. This is vital for the king's afterlife.

Step 6 Wash body and cover in natron for forty days.

Step 7 Stuff the body with rags to ensure it keeps its shape. Before winding clean linen rags around it, replace any lost limbs with wooden versions (feel free to replace the eyes with onions or polished black stones) so the body is complete in the afterlife.

Step 8 Complete the bandaging process, adding lucky charms or gold and jewellery to the mummy.

Step 9 Put the stomach, lungs, intestines and liver in their own canopic jars. Add natron for preservation and seal them.

Step 10 Lastly and most importantly, don't forget to open the mummy's mouth. This is a vital ceremony and will ensure the pharaoh can eat, drink and breathe in the afterlife.

Chapter 7

LIFTING THE LID ON
TUTANKHAMUN'S COFFIN

So now the pharaoh has been mummified, you're ready to put him in his tomb, right?

Wrong. There were still lots of things to do before the body could be buried properly. Until the discovery of Tutankhamun, archaeologists had never found the intact coffin of a pharaoh and the amazing finds they uncovered helped to lift the lid on the burial secrets of Tutankhamun.

Before they could reach Tutankhamun's body, archaeologists uncovered three shrines one on top of the other. All the shrines were coated in gold and ornately decorated.

Below the third shrine was a sarcophagus – a stone coffin – carved out of hard rock called quartzite with a yellow painted lid. Within the sarcophagus was another coffin and inside this was another, smaller coffin.

Finally, inside this coffin, archaeologists discovered a mummy wearing a solid gold mask. At last, they had reached Tutankhamun's body.

MUMMY–MANIA

For thousands of years, mummies have fascinated people. Having seen them in museums, in books or on TV, most people think they may know a lot about them – but do they? Why not test someone you know with our true or false quiz...

1. The word 'mummy' is derived from the Arab word meaning 'body'.
2. One king of England thought he would achieve greatness by rubbing powdered mummy on himself.

3. Parts of mummies have been used as medicine.

Take one part of Mummy 3 times a day

4. The Duke of Hamilton had a strange request in his will. He wanted his hand mummified after his death.

ANSWERS

1. False.

Mummy actually comes from the Arab word 'mammia' that means bitumen. They were given this name because when some mummies were discovered, they had a dark black appearance and it was wrongly thought they were coated in this tar-like substance.

2. True.

King Charles II thought it a right royal wheeze to rub mummy powder onto his skin.

3. True.

For hundreds of years, doctors prescribed chopped up mummies to cure everything from broken bones to the flu.

4. False.

In fact, the dotty duke decided to have his whole body mummified. His final wish was respected after his death in 1852 and his mummified remains were placed in an Egyptian stone coffin.

UNRAVELLING THE MYSTERIES OF THE MUMMIES

It's thanks to the mummies that historians have been able to discover the facts about the lives of some Egyptians.

GRAND UNWRAPPING OF
THE MUMMY

STARRING: DR PETTIGREW

NOW PLAYING AT:

THE ROYAL COLLEGE OF SURGEONS

CERTIFICATE: 18 AND OVER

"THIS SHOW IS SET TO RUN AND RUN!"

Refreshments will be served after the performance

The skills of the ancient Egyptian embalmers meant that many bodies were amazingly well preserved and they could be studied thousands of years later. Mummy mania was so high around the turn of the century that unwrapping mummies became more like show business than archaeology.

On one occasion, the members of the audience who came to see Dr Pettigrew's unwrappings were in for an extra shock.

Was it because..?

A. One of the mummies came alive

B. One of the mummies turned out to be a fake

C. One of the mummies turned out to have a wooden leg

Answer: B.

A. There is no record of mummies ever coming to life – except in Hollywood movies.

B. Enterprising Egyptians often used to make fake mummies made from rags and bits of fresh corpses in order to sell them to tourists. It's even been rumoured that the business was so profitable that fake mummy factories operated.

C. The embalmers weren't pulling anyone's leg with this one. If a leg had been lost or had rotted away during embalming, they would often replace it with a wooden limb.

DID YOU KNOW...?

The last unwrapping of a mummy was carried out in 1975 in Manchester. It was the first for over 70 years and was performed by a team of experts using specialist medical equipment to examine the patient... er mummy.

Nowadays, examining a mummy is done in a much more scientific (and to be honest, slightly more dull) way. Mummies aren't unwrapped but are X-rayed or put into a CAT scan. Studies have revealed some fascinating facts about how the ancient Egyptians lived... and died.

Fascinating Fact 1 Archaeologists discovered that most ancient Egyptians had severe teething troubles. The reason was that even though they had over 65 varieties of bread, it was so coarse that it ground their teeth down to their gums.

Fascinating Fact 2 A study of bones revealed that the Egyptians suffered from similar diseases such as arthritis, gout and rheumatism that we do.

Fascinating Fact 3 Pharaoh Rameses III was a big leader in more than one way. His mummy reveals that he was very fat when he died.

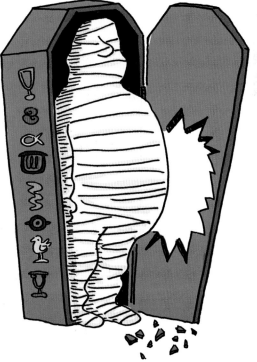

71

TUTANKHAMUN – A MURDERED MUMMY?

When it came to examining the mummified remains of Tutankhamun, historians were in for a double whammy of surprises. First of all, archaeologists discovered that he was only about nineteen when he died but even more importantly, his skull revealed that he had received a severe blow to the head.

Could Tutankhamun have been killed? Who could have dunnit? It was time to launch a murder enquiry.

Victim's name: Tutankhamun

Cause of death: sudden blow to the head.

Prime suspect: the person who succeeded Tutankhamun to the throne: his uncle Ay.

Motive: if Tutankhamun was murdered, the reasons might lie with his father, Akhenaten.

Akhenaten was an extraordinary pharaoh who had the extraordinary idea to do away with all the gods except Aten, the sun-god. To support his religious revolution, he closed the old temples and moved the court to a brand new city in the middle of the desert. This new city was dedicated to Aten and was designed in a completely new style with wide streets and single-storey houses. New styles of painting and sculpting were also introduced.

As you can imagine, these changes had upset quite a few people – in fact, almost everyone in Egyptian society. When Akhenaten died, the mysterious king called Ankhkhprerue Smenkhkaredjerkhepru came to power and continued Akhenaten's revolution.

Throughout this period of change, one figure was present. Tutankhamun's uncle, Ay, was the most senior figure at the royal court. When Akhenaten and his successor died, the dynasty passed into the hands of a nine year old boy – but perhaps real power lay with his uncle.

Certainly, Akenaten's revolution failed. Aten was abandoned and the old temples and gods were worshipped as before. As a boy, Tutankhamun would never have been able to challenge his uncle, but what about as a nineteen year old man? Would he be so keen to listen to good old Uncle Ay? Uncle Ay was used to his position of power and he wouldn't have been so keen to give it up. However, perhaps there was a simple solution – to murder his nephew and take the throne instead.

Evidence: Ay certainly followed Tutankhamun to the throne but did he get his nephew out of the way first? All the sleuthing done by archaeologists is based on a hunch but nothing more. Conclusive proof will probably never be found one way or another so it's up to you to decide if you think the boy king was murdered.

Chapter 8

EGYPT-MANIA

The discovery of Tutankhamun's tomb unleashed a severe case of Egypt-mania. Throughout Europe and America, interest in the boy king and his fellow pharaohs became more fashionable than ever before and shows no sign of dying down to this day.

The treasures of Tutankhamun helped archaeologists spill the beans on life during his reign. His tomb helped lift the lid on Egyptian burials and attitudes to the afterlife while examining his mummy may lead to dishing the dirt on a mysterious murder.

Tutankhamun hardly made an impact during his short reign but he continues to have a huge impact today and not just because of what was found in his tomb.

The reason for Tutankhamun's continuing popularity lies in the story of the Pharaoh's Curse. To get the inside track on the curse, let's step back in time to that moment when Howard Carter and Lord Carnarvon were standing in front of the unopened tomb. Were they about to unleash an ancient curse, a terrible revenge for disturbing the three-thousand-year sleep of a pharaoh?

For almost a year after the tomb had been opened, everything seemed normal but then Lord Carnarvon died of an infected mosquito bite and sparked a series of strange stories.

A sudden sandstorm blew up as the last people left the tomb and a hawk – the sign of the pharaohs – was seen hovering in the west.

A physic was quoted as predicting that anyone who entered the tomb would suffer "dire punishment".

On the day of Carnarvon's death, there was a black-out in Cairo and his dog howled then died itself.

For the next two decades, the death of anyone connected with the tomb was reported to be caused by the mummy's curse.

But, if there had been a curse, surely Howard Carter would have been struck down. In fact, he ignored the whole business and got on with archaeology until he was sixty-four when he died of a heart attack.

Yet, some people still can't forget the curse, and in the sixties it hit the headlines once again, when an Egyptian museum keeper dreamt he would die if he allowed Tutankhamun's treasures to leave the country. Unfortunately, the treasures were about to be loaned to France for an exhibition and the keeper's arguments were in vain. After the final meeting, he left the museum, was hit by a car and died within two days.

So what do you think? In the end, the Curse of the Mummy – like the mystery of Tutankhamun's death – is one of the things that no

one can dish the dirt on. And yet, perhaps buried beneath the desert
sands of Egypt lies another undisturbed tomb just waiting to be
discovered and to spill the beans on more secrets of the lives of the
pharaohs.

WRITE LIKE AN EGYPTIAN

See if you can write your own secret messages using these hieroglyphs...

The alphabet:

	= A	~~~~	= N	
	= B		= O	
	= C	☐	= P	
	= D	◁	= Q	
	= E/I	⬭	= R	
	= F	—ǁ—	= S	
	= G	⌓	= T	
	= H	⊚	= U	
	= J		= V	
	= K		= W	
	= L		= X	
	= M	ǀǀ	= Y	

Ⱡ = Z

Basic numbers:

ǀ	= 1
∩	= 10
⟲	= 100
	= 1,000
	= 10,000

Chapter 1

FAMILY ALBUM

Julius Caesar was born in Rome in 100BC. His father was a not very successful politician, but Caesar came from a very grand family. Caesar's family tree includes:

- at least two murderers
- two murder victims
- six soldiers
- two major gods.

Caesar followed in the family footsteps – he became all four.

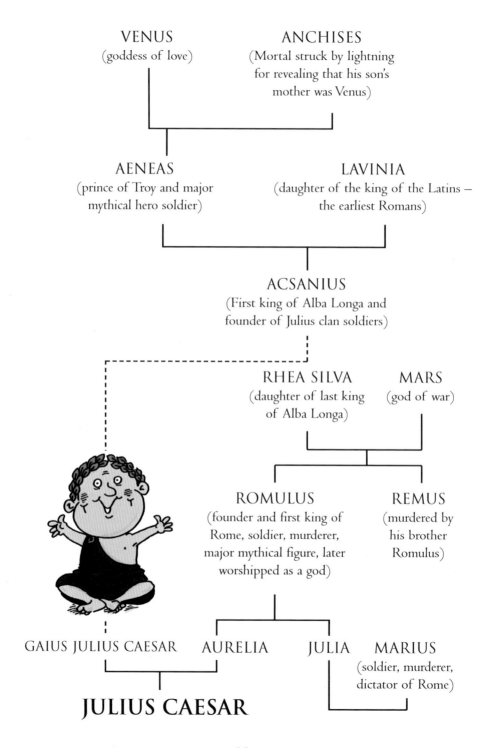

VENUS
(goddess of love)

ANCHISES
(Mortal struck by lightning
for revealing that his son's
mother was Venus)

AENEAS
(prince of Troy and major
mythical hero soldier)

LAVINIA
(daughter of the king of the Latins –
the earliest Romans)

ACSANIUS
(First king of Alba Longa and
founder of Julius clan soldiers)

RHEA SILVA
(daughter of last king
of Alba Longa)

MARS
(god of war)

ROMULUS
(founder and first king of
Rome, soldier, murderer,
major mythical figure, later
worshipped as a god)

REMUS
(murdered by
his brother
Romulus)

GAIUS JULIUS CAESAR   AURELIA   JULIA   MARIUS
(soldier, murderer,
dictator of Rome)

JULIUS CAESAR

HOME TOWN

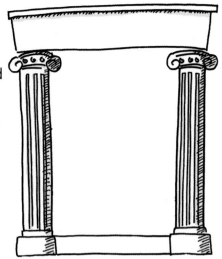

Rome in 100BC was the biggest and most important city in the world, and Caesar's family was one of the oldest and most respected families in Rome. Caesar's father was a senator, a member of the council or parliament of wealthy Romans who ran the Roman empire.

Rome at this time did not have an emperor or a king. The Roman empire was a republic – that means it was a nation without a monarch. Every year the Senate elected two consuls whose jobs were to be something like joint prime ministers for a year. The other ministers were elected, too.

All male citizens present in Rome at the time of an election could vote. In cases of emergency – like war or revolution – the Senate could appoint a dictator (a supreme commander) to take charge, but only for six months.

The baby Caesar would one day change all that. Although he would never have the title, he would grow up to be, in all but name, the first Roman emperor.

FAMILY STORIES

No-one knew exactly when the city of Rome was founded, but there were a number of stories which children like the young Caesar were told. One of these stories told how twins Romulus and Remus were left to die when they were babies by their wicked uncle. A wild wolf found them and brought them up. When they were adults, and Romulus started to build a city, Remus made fun of him by jumping over the city walls. Romulus got so cross that he lost his temper and killed his brother. Romulus carried on building his city which he named after himself – Rome. This was an important story for Caesar's family because Caesar's mother claimed to be directly descended from Romulus.

But an even more important story to the Caesar family was the story of Aeneas. Caesar's father claimed descent back to Aeneas himself, the great hero and a son of a goddess. Aeneas, a prince from the city of Troy, had sailed to Italy and founded a kingdom which was the beginning of the Roman empire.

Here's the story that Caesar would have been told when he was a child, about Aeneas and the Trojan War. It's one of the oldest and strangest stories in the world.

THE TROJAN WAR AND PRINCE AENEAS

Over a thousand years before you (Caesar) were born, a great war was fought at a city called Troy (it's on the coast of what is now Turkey).

The war started when Paris, one of the sons of the King of Troy, kidnapped Helen, the wife of Menelaus who was the king of a town called Sparta in Greece. Paris took Helen back to Troy to be his wife.

Menelaus was very annoyed because:

> (a) Helen was young.
> (b) Helen was very beautiful.
> (c) Menelaus was old, ugly and bad-tempered and was very unlikely to find a wife as good-looking as Helen again.
> (d) Menelaus was very proud, and knew he'd been made to look a fool.

Helen didn't mind being kidnapped. Helen was in love with Paris because:

> (a) Paris was young.
> (b) Paris was handsome.
> (c) Paris was being helped by Venus, the goddess of love – sneaky Paris!

Menelaus persuaded the other Greek kings like

Agamemnon, King of Athens – the most powerful man in the world; Odysseus, King of Ithaca – the cleverest man in the world; and Achilles, King of the Myrmidons – the best fighter in the world; to help him start a war to get Helen back. (The Spartans were famous for wanting to solve every problem by fighting).

You would have thought with a team like that, it wouldn't have taken long to get Helen back. So did the Greeks. They were wrong.

The Greek army sailed to Troy, then they camped outside the city walls and waited for the Trojans to get:

(a) scared
(b) hungry
(c) bored

and give Helen back.

They waited... and they waited... and they waited. Every few days, some Trojan soldiers would leave the city and fight some of the Greek soldiers. But when it got dark, the Trojans went home to their city and the Greeks went back to their camp.

This went on for ten years, until Odysseus had a brilliant idea.

One morning the Trojans woke up to find that the Greeks had sailed away. All that was left, where the Greek camp had been, was an enormous wooden horse.

What a trophy! The biggest toy horse in the world! The triumphant Trojans dragged the horse into the city, and began the celebrations.

That night, when all the Trojans were either asleep or drunk, a trapdoor opened in the horse and out climbed a troop of Greek soldiers. They crept to the gates of the city and opened them.

The Greek army was outside waiting for the gates to open. They hadn't sailed away, but just sailed out of sight.

They burnt Troy to the ground, killing the men and boys, and carrying off the women as slaves.

Well... they didn't kill all the men. Aeneas, Paris's cousin and the son of the goddess Venus, escaped on a boat with a handful of followers. They sailed to Italy, where Aeneas married Lavinia, the daughter of the king of the Latins.

Aeneas and Lavinia had a son, Ascanius, who founded the city of Alba Longa, from which grew the whole Roman empire. Ascanius also took the family name of 'Julius'.

So that was the story. You probably noticed that Aeneas was supposed to have been the son of the goddess Venus. That was why Caesar's family not only claimed they were the descendants of Aeneas, but also claimed to be related to the goddess Venus, too.

Chapter 2

BABY IN DANGER

The Romans had many customs which we would say were cruel, and because of one of these customs, Caesar's life was in great danger as soon as he was born.

According to an ancient tradition, Caesar's mother, Aurelia, had to lay her new-born baby at his father's feet. If Caesar's father picked him up, everything was fine; if he refused, the baby would be taken to a public place like the side of a road – and left. If a kind-hearted passer-by didn't pick up the baby it would die within hours.

For a moment or two there must have been an anxious silence in the room, until... Gaius picked up his son!

Nine days later, Caesar's parents held a naming ceremony, which is similar to a christening. Friends and relatives of Gaius and Aurelia came to the house with gifts, incense was burnt, the baby was bathed and then given his name: Gaius Julius Caesar, just like his father. *Gaius* was his personal name like Gary, or Michael or Peter. *Julius* was the old family name, the clan name for everyone – cousins, second cousins, third and fourth cousins and so on – who claimed to be related to Aeneas and his son.

Caesar was the surname of their particular family, and it comes from an ancient word for *elephant*. There was a story behind that too.

A hundred years before Caesar was born, a general called Hannibal invaded Italy. Hannibal came from a place called Carthage, in North Africa, and as well as bringing lots of soldiers with him – a good idea if you're fighting a war – he brought with him a secret weapon which he hoped would absolutely *terrify* the Romans – battle elephants!

One of Caesar's ancestors had single-handedly killed one of Hannibal's elephants in a battle and had either taken or been given the name *Caesar* – the elephant killer. The name stuck, as nicknames often do, and became his family name.

GROWING UP ROMAN

When he was a baby and a toddler Caesar was looked after by a nurse, just as rich children today may be looked after by a nanny or nursery maid.

Then, when he was seven, Caesar started his schooling. But Caesar never went to school. He took all his lessons at home.

Caesar's first teachers were his parents. His mother taught him to read and write both Latin and Greek. Latin was the language of the Romans, but Greek was very important too, because a lot of Roman culture – art, history, philosophy and religion – had been taken from the Greeks. She also taught him his first lessons in public speaking.

Public speaking, or to give it its Greek name, *rhetoric,* was a very important part of any aristocratic Roman's education. All the best jobs in Rome – like being Consul – were elected. To get a good job, you had to be able to persuade people to vote for you. Rhetoric was the art of persuasion.

Caesar's father taught him physical skills like wrestling, throwing the javelin and discus, and swimming. But these weren't simply sports; this was training for the army. Caesar's father knew that, like all high-born Romans, someday young Caesar would join the army. The skills he learnt as a boy might someday be the difference between life and death.

Young Caesar was a natural athlete, and he especially enjoyed riding. When he was in his early teens he often spent his afternoons, after his lessons had finished, at a huge sports ground called the *Campus Martius.* Caesar was a bit of a show-off and used to ride across the sports ground as fast as he could with no hands.

After a few years of lessons from his parents, young Caesar started lessons with a tutor, a Greek slave who taught him grammar, literature, and more classes on how to win friends and influence people through making speeches.

This seems a good place to tell you about...

SLAVES, PLEBS, KNIGHTS AND PATRICIANS

In ancient Rome there were rules and customs for everything, and everyone belonged to one of four classes.

Patricians – top dogs

At the top were the families like Caesar's who were known as *patricians*. They were similar to the old 'noble' families of Britain – the dukes, earls and lords. They had land and money, and some had the right by birth to a place in the Senate (like British aristocrats used to have a seat in Parliament in the House of Lords). The patricians believed they had a right to run the country. They also thought that doing ordinary jobs was for the lower orders. Like the Caesar family, the other patrician families claimed they were descended from the original founders of Rome.

Equites (knights) – almost pedigree dogs

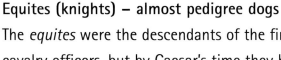

The *equites* were the descendants of the first Roman cavalry officers, but by Caesar's time they had nothing to do with horses. Equite was just a title, like a modern British knighthood (no-one expects Sir Elton John or Sir Paul McCartney to ride around on horseback wearing armour, although the title comes from a time when that's what knights did).

Like many British knights today, Roman equites in Caesar's time were businessmen – rich merchants, bankers and money-lenders. Patricians thought it was beneath them to lend money, but they were only too happy to borrow it – often vast sums. During Caesar's lifetime, the equites were becoming more and more powerful. Equites could be elected to the Senate.

Plebeians – working dogs

These were the ordinary working people, craftsmen and shop keepers. They were full citizens and could vote in elections. They also elected two special representatives called *tribunes* who could veto any law passed by the Senate. That meant that if a tribune didn't like a law it would be thrown out. No-one else in Rome had the power to overrule the Senate.

Slaves – mutts and curs

It may seem strange that an important family like Caesar's would have had their son educated by a slave, but that's how things were done in Rome. Slaves did an awful lot of the work.

As you might expect, slaves did all the hard, horrible jobs that no-one else wanted to do, like mining or breaking rocks in quarries. There were household slaves to do all the housework like cooking and cleaning. By the time Caesar was a boy, more and more jobs in Rome were done by slaves. A lot of what we would call 'office workers' – secretaries, clerks and accountants – were slaves. Slaves also did jobs which we would call 'professional' – most librarians, teachers and doctors were also slaves. And entertainers, like dancers and singers, were slaves too. Slaves earned money, and if they saved enough they could buy their freedom.

But however trusted and even well-paid a slave was, he or she was not regarded as a person, but as the property of their master. And that master could, in theory, do what he liked with them. Sometimes they did. Pliny, a Roman writer recorded:

> **Vedius Pollio [a friend of Caesar's nephew] practised his barbarity with the assistance of moray eels, into whose tank he threw condemned slaves... because with no other living creature could he watch a man being torn to pieces utterly and instantaneously.**

Slave marriages were not recognised, and any children born to slaves automatically became slaves themselves. Although masters as cruel as Vedius Pollio were rare, Roman law laid down brutal punishments for slaves who committed crimes. If, for example, a slave killed his master, even someone as cruel as Vedius Pollio, *all* the slaves in the house would be executed.

UNEMPLOYED – DOGS FOR SALE

Because so many jobs were done by slaves, lots of plebeians, equites and even patricians had no work and no money. During Caesar's lifetime there were about 500,000 people living in Rome. Around 130,000 people received free food – what the Romans called the *corn dole.* These would have been plebeians. The higher class unemployed would have taken up being 'clients'. Clients were what might be called high class scroungers, living on what they could get as handouts from rich senators. Every rich man had a group of clients, and every client had a 'patron', a particular rich man who looked after him.

Everyday at dawn, a huge army of clients would put on their togas and start queuing outside the houses of their patrons. The queue would be in strict order of class: patrician relatives of the rich man first, followed by non-related patricians, then equites and so on. When the rich man came out – to go to the Senate, for example – he would give out gifts of money or even food, to his clients.

Why did the rich man do this? Out of kindness? No. The clients, and the unemployed plebeians on the corn dole, had something a rich and powerful man needed in order to stay rich: **VOTES**.

The unemployed plebeians and the higher-class clients were all citizens and therefore had the right to vote in the elections for all the top jobs. In return for being a patron, the rich man got the votes of his clients. It was as simple as that.

A rich man could also try to buy the votes of the plebeians, by voting for increases in the corn dole, and paying for the entertainments – like gladiator fights, or fights between men and exotic wild animals – that filled the days of the un- and underemployed. The Romans used to call this giving the people "bread and circuses". Any patrician who seemed to stand up for the common man, especially of the idle sort, could have a huge number of votes in his pocket. The only trouble was, it all cost a *fortune!*

Chapter 3

ADULT LIFE STARTS
WITH A TOGA

When he was fifteen, Caesar's father gave him his *toga virilis* – his adult toga. This was a big day in a boy's life. Like an 18th birthday nowadays, or graduation from school or college, it was the start of adult life.

The toga was a huge piece of circular woollen cloth, like an enormous curved blanket. It was five-and-a-half metres wide, and was worn draped and folded over a tunic. The toga was so big that it was virtually impossible to put on without the help of at least one slave, and it was usually worn with only a belt to hold it together. It was a major problem to walk, or move in any way, without the whole thing coming unwrapped.

It was the official dress – the business suit or uniform – of the adult male Roman citizen, and only *full* citizens of the Roman empire were allowed to wear it.

Senators were allowed to wear a toga with a purple stripe along the edge to show their rank, rather like a corporal or sergeant in the army now wears stripes to show they're above the ordinary soldier.

When a boy got his toga it showed that he'd become a man, and the day he received it there would be a mixture of a party and a religious celebration.

Caesar's special day started with friends and relations coming to the house to congratulate him and give him presents. Then Caesar walked with his father to the temple of Jupiter, made a sacrifice and was officially proclaimed a full citizen of the Roman Empire.

Caesar was very keen on fashion, and soon developed his own form of the toga. He added wrist-length fringed sleeves and always wore his belt very slack. One of his family's greatest political enemies, Sulla, when seeing Caesar wearing his fancy toga, was heard to mutter: 'Beware of that boy with his loose clothes.'

MORE TO BEING A GROWN-UP THAN JUST A BLANKET

There was only one way for a boy of Caesar's class to get on in Rome, and that was to go into politics.

None of the best jobs in the Roman Empire – as a lawyer or judge, top civil servant, religious leader or senior officer in the army – were permanent jobs. They were all elected for short terms. (In the same way that today, in the United States, jobs like district attorney, chief-of-police, sheriff or fire-chief in towns and cities are also elected. The commander-in-chief of the US army is also elected – that's the president.) Nowadays we think of these as separate careers, needing particular skills and training. But in Caesar's day, an aristocratic Roman would move from one job to another without thinking too much about it.

He might start out as a junior lawyer, then go into the army – as an officer, of course. After a year or two in the army, he might

CAESAR

CONSUL
MURDER
CORRUPTION
INTRIGUE
INTER-MARRIAGE
GENERAL
PRIEST
BRIBERY
JUNIOR MINISTER
SOLDIER
JUNIOR LAWYER

CAREER ·STEPS·

try a year as a judge or a junior minister. Then, if he bribed enough people, he could get elected as a religious leader, even a chief priest, or he could then go back into the army, this time as a general. If he fought a successful war, and if he was really lucky, he might come back to Rome and be elected as one of the two consuls who were chosen every year to rule the empire.

Does that sound strange? Well, that was the sort of career that ambitious young Romans like Caesar hoped for.

So in order to get one of these jobs, Caesar had to become a politician. And at the age of 15, with a family like his, Caesar might have assumed success was guaranteed. But it wasn't.

A BRIGHT START

Success for a patrician didn't depend on how clever you were, but on who your family and friends were. Did you have a rich father, or uncle who could help you buy the votes you needed? Did you have a father-in-law or older brother who could call in favours in order to get you the job you wanted?

We would say today, and quite rightly, that the whole system was completely rotten and corrupt. But for the Romans this was how things had always been, and as far as they were concerned this was how things always would be.

Caesar's father wasn't rich or powerful, but his Uncle Marius, who was married to Caesar's Aunt Julia, was the most powerful man in the whole Roman empire.

MARIUS

Uncle Marius was a very unusual man. He wasn't born a patrician, but had worked his way up through the army through sheer ability and ruthlessness. Uncle Marius was brilliant, Uncle Marius was charming, and Uncle Marius was quite prepared to use murder to get his way if his brilliance and his charm didn't get him what he wanted.

Marius had utterly transformed the Roman army. Until Marius became a general, only people who owned land and had enough money to provide all their own equipment were allowed to join the army. Marius changed the rules so that any citizen could join. Soldiers now had their equipment provided for them, had reasonable pay, and the promise of a pension – either money or a small plot of land – when they finished their twenty years service.

Suddenly, thousands of unemployed men could have a job, a wage, and the hope of a secure future for themselves and their families by joining the army. The ordinary people thought Marius was great, especially as he claimed to be one of them. And the soldiers in his army were so grateful, they would follow him to hell and back.

Marius became not just a soldier, but one of the most powerful politicians in the empire. He was the leader of a group of senators called the *populares* who claimed to be the champions of the ordinary people. Caesar's father was a *popularis*, too.

But powerful men make powerful enemies, and Marius had made a very powerful enemy, a man named Sulla. Sulla had once been Marius's lieutenant, but had later become one of the leaders of the other main group in the Senate, the *optimates*. The optimates supported the aristocrats, not the ordinary people. They tried to pass laws to give more power to the patricians – the land-owners and the rich.

Then in 87BC, when Caesar was 13, Marius and his ally Cinna seized power in Rome while Sulla was away fighting in Greece. Marius was appointed dictator and at once ordered the execution of Sulla's main supporters.

Sulla was a powerful man, with a long memory. But Sulla was in exile a long way away. For Marius's family and friends – including Caesar and his family – the future looked bright.

Chapter 4

DISASTERS FOR CAESAR

Caesar's father should have helped him on his way to the start of his career, but just before Caesar was 16 his father died. Caesar was now the head of his family. Soon after, there was another loss for the family, when Marius died too.

Caesar wasn't sure what to do, or where to turn for the help his father and his uncle would have given him. Then Aunt Julia stepped in.

Marius's widow was a very strong woman; no-one argued with Aunt Julia. Young Caesar was already engaged to be married to Cossetta, the daughter of a wealthy equite who could lend Caesar the money he needed to get a start in politics. But that was nothing compared to what Aunt Julia had in mind.

Caesar didn't marry Cossetta. Cossetta got dumped. Instead Caesar married Cornelia, the daughter of Cinna, Uncle Marius's old ally and now the most powerful man in Rome.

A brilliant future now seemed certain for young Caesar. Then, another disaster – his father-in-law Cinna was killed in Spain during a mutiny of his troops.

During the time that Marius and Cinna were in power, Sulla had been in exile, waiting for his chance. This was it. Sulla didn't hesitate. Within days he'd marched back to Rome and seized power. Caesar was in deep trouble.

If success depended on family connections rather than anything you did, so could your life. Sulla was back, and he had a list of everyone he considered an enemy: anyone who had opposed him, or anyone who was related to them. Caesar was Marius's nephew and Cinna's son-in-law. To Sulla, even though Caesar was hardly more than a boy, he was one of the most dangerous men in Rome. Caesar was arrested immediately and taken to Sulla.

Sulla had set up his headquarters in the temple of the war goddess Bellona. Not far away, on the Campus Martius, supporters of Marius were being put to death. Their screams could clearly be heard from the room in which Caesar was questioned. Imagine

how frightening this must have been for Caesar. Would he be the next to be marched out to the Campus Martius?

But instead of condemning him immediately, Sulla offered Caesar a deal. "Join me," he said, "and, to show you're on my side, divorce your wife and I'll pick you a new one."

Ninety-nine out of a hundred Romans, with their life in such danger, would have taken Sulla's offer. Not Caesar.
He refused.

Sulla must have been astonished at the teenager's refusal, because he didn't have him killed at once. Instead, he confiscated everything that Caesar and his wife owned and let Caesar go.

It didn't take Sulla long to have second thoughts. He declared Caesar an outlaw, with a price on his head. But when the first bounty hunters arrived at his house to kill him, Caesar was gone.

ON THE RUN

This is what the Roman writer Appian said in his book on the civil wars:

> Sulla... pronounced a sentence of death on forty senators and about 1,600 knights... Very soon he added other senators to the list. Some of them, caught unawares, were killed where they were found; at home, in the street, or in the temple... Others were dragged through the streets and kicked to death, the spectators being too frightened to

> utter a word of protest at the horrors they witnessed. Others were expelled from Rome or had their property and belongings confiscated. Spies were looking everywhere for those who had fled the city, and killing any they caught leaving.

For a whole year Caesar was in hiding in the countryside outside Rome. He often had to go from one hiding place to another at night to avoid Sulla's spies who were looking for him. During this time Caesar became so ill with malaria that he sometimes had to be carried from one hiding place to another by friends.

Once, he was actually caught by a group of Sulla's men, but managed to borrow enough money to bribe them to go away.

Meanwhile in Rome, his mother, his wife and the rest of his family were begging Sulla to let him come back. Eventually, Sulla gave in. But Caesar didn't trust Sulla. Instead of coming home to Rome, Caesar joined the army and didn't return to Rome until 78BC when he got news that Sulla was dead.

ARMY LIFE

The Roman army was divided into legions, roughly equivalent to the regiments of the modern British army. Each legion had a number and title – for example *The Ninth Hispania* – and each legion had a standard, a silver eagle which was carried into battle with them. If the enemy captured the eagle it was a great disgrace, and the legion would be disbanded if they couldn't win it back.

Each legion was made up of nine cohorts of 480 men each. Caesar's first job would have been as the officer in charge of a cohort.

Even in peacetime, army life was tough. Every day the troops had to practice swimming, running and javelin throwing, and every couple of weeks they would have to march at least thirty kilometres in a day at speeds of up to eight kilometres per hour.

Fighting wasn't the only job of the legions. They were also responsible for building roads and bridges. So as well as all their weapons, food and cooking pots, each soldier had to carry digging tools with him.

Caesar's Uncle Marius invented a forked pole to help the

legionnaires carry all their equipment. It may have helped the soldiers, but it got them the nickname "Marius's mules".

Many people hated life in the army, but Caesar loved it. He was strong and fit, and discovered that not only was he a good fighter, but he was a natural leader – other soldiers respected him and would willingly follow him.

Chapter 5

HARD LESSONS

The Caesar who came home to Rome in 78BC wasn't a boy any more. He was only in his early twenties, but he was a tough survivor. He'd survived a civil war, he'd survived being an outlaw on the run, and he'd not just survived but *enjoyed* the tough life of the army. He'd seen the violence and killing of Sulla's dictatorship, and could probably remember the killings which his Uncle Marius had ordered when he'd seized control of Rome. If what he'd learned had to be summed up in one phrase it was: *trust no-one, especially not the Senate.*

Caesar knew that the only safe place to be was at the very top. And that's where he decided he was going.

To get to the top in Roman politics took money, *lots* of money. Caesar needed money to bribe senators, money to bribe equites, and money to bribe the ordinary people of Rome. But that wasn't all. Caesar knew that to get to the top he needed soldiers who would do *anything* he asked them to do – that was another lesson he'd learnt from his Uncle Marius. That took money too. But Caesar didn't have money. What could he do?

Easy: he borrowed. He borrowed a fortune, from anyone who would lend it to him. He even borrowed money to make himself look rich, so that he could borrow *even more* money.

"Lend me money now, and when I'm the most powerful man in Rome you'll get back hundreds of times the value of what you lend me today!" – that was the deal that Caesar offered. The tough young man must have been convincing, because there were plenty of Romans willing to lend money to young Caesar.

The first thing Caesar did was to try and make his name as a lawyer and a public speaker. He lost both his first cases, but made such an impression that the accused men hired the best lawyers in Rome to defend themselves against him.

Caesar was now famous. Among lawyers and politicians, he was famous as a brilliant lawyer and speaker. Among ordinary people he was famous for his generosity to his clients and the lavish parties he threw (with borrowed money, of course). If there had been gossip columns in Rome, Caesar would have been in them every day:

SALVE!

THE CELEBRITY MAGAZINE WITH AN EAR TO THE FORUM

Another wild night at the home of free-spending young swinger, Gaius Julius Caesar.

Having made a name for himself as a lawyer with a big future, Caesar was throwing another of his extravagant parties – this time to say farewell to a few close friends before setting sail for Greece.

Caesar hasn't gotta lotta loot, but he still manages to push the boat out –

using other people's cash!

But one thing's for sure, Caesar's got his eye on the top job. So, it'll be spend, spend, spend – and lend, lend, lend – for this partying patrician!

Caesar's Parties are great.... but can we afford them?

ON PAGE 16 – Crassus, Rome's No. 1 builder, shows SALVE readers round his own lovely home.

But Caesar's creditors, the people who had lent him money, were getting impatient; so impatient that some of them were asking for their money back *or else.*

Caesar gave the moneylenders the slip, and sailed for Greece. Greece was a good choice. He'd become famous by standing up for Greeks against corrupt Roman officials, and certain Greeks had hinted that they might reward Caesar with what Caesar needed most – money. Greece also had the best teachers of rhetoric. While in Greece, Caesar hoped to study with one of them. The next time he went to court, he *wasn't* going to lose again.

Everything was looking good; everything was going to plan. The boat was making good progress, only a couple more days and... Caesar looked out to sea. Other ships were approaching fast. Pirate ships.

CAPTURED BY PIRATES

The Mediterranean Sea at this time was being terrorised by pirates. They would stop ships and steal their cargoes, and any wealthy passengers would be held to ransom. That's what happened to Caesar.

Most people would have been terrified at being captured by pirates, but Caesar seemed to treat the whole experience as a huge joke. Plutarch, the Greek historian, wrote:

> **When the pirates demanded a ransom of twenty talents Caesar burst out laughing. They did not know, he said, who it was they had captured – and he volunteered to pay them fifty.**

The pirates let some of Caesar's companions go ashore to start collecting the ransom money. Caesar, of course, stayed behind as a hostage. Even then, with his friends gone, Caesar didn't seem in the least bit nervous. He treated the pirates like servants. Once, when his afternoon nap was disturbed, he yelled at the pirates to be quiet.

Oi! Seadogs, less of your yapping!

> For 38 days... he joined in all their games and exercises, just as if he were their leader instead of their prisoner. He also wrote poems and speeches which he read aloud to them, and if they failed to admire his work, he would call them illiterate savages to their faces, and would often laughingly threaten to have them all hanged.

Caesar may have been laughing, but he wasn't joking. Caesar was a proud man, and he was planning to be a successful soldier and politician. He couldn't be seen to come off second best to a group of pirates.

When the ransom was paid and Caesar was freed, he immediately borrowed even more money, chartered a small fleet of ships, found the pirates and captured them.

He took them ashore and demanded justice from the local Greek magistrates. When the magistrates dithered – maybe because they were afraid of the pirates – Caesar marched the prisoners out and crucified them all. (But because he'd enjoyed their company, he had them strangled first rather than leave them to a slow, agonising death. That was Caesar's idea of mercy.)

Maybe this adventure shows another of the lessons Caesar may have learned from Marius and Sulla: *Never let anyone get the better of you, and treat any enemy without mercy.*

Caesar returned to Rome. The story of his adventures with the pirates added to his growing reputation. Here was a young man, people said, who was not only a good lawyer, but was brave, strong and ruthless. The sort of person, they whispered, that Rome needed to bring order to the chaos caused by the bickering, back-stabbing, indecisive senators.

Chapter 6

ROME IN TURMOIL

The Senate had never been designed to run an empire. It was a town council which, by accident, found itself trying to run half the world. Rome was in a dreadful mess.

More and more people came to Rome looking for work and finding none. The most important jobs in government were bought and sold, while the generals who commanded the armies overseas became more and more powerful, and more and more ambitious.

The Senate desperately need to reorganise itself, but the two groups or parties – the *optimates* and the *populares* – had utterly opposite views of what needed to be done. "More power to the rich and powerful!" yelled the optimates. "More power to the people!" bellowed the populares. There was no agreement, so nothing changed.

Elections had become street battles between the supporters of rival candidates. Plutarch, a Greek writer, wrote:

> Candidates for office quite shamelessly bribed the electorate... people who received bribes went down to the Forum [the main square in Rome where elections were held] not so much to vote for their benefactors as to fight for them with bows and arrows and swords and slings. Often, before an election was over, the place where it had been held was stained with blood and defiled with dead bodies.

Caesar borrowed more and more money and bribed more and more important people to try and get a really important job. And when money wasn't enough to win over an important backer, Caesar was quite prepared to crawl and fawn. According to Cassius Dio, a Roman historian: "Caesar showed himself perfectly ready to serve and flatter everybody, even ordinary persons... he did not mind temporarily grovelling."

But all the bribery and flattery worked: Caesar got the job he wanted, as a *quaestor,* one of twenty magistrates and administrators who helped to run the empire. Caesar was sent to Spain to help the Roman governor.

But not everything was going well. Cornelia died before he was due to go to Spain. Caesar was without a wife, and his young daughter Julia had lost her mother.

ONWARDS AND UPWARDS

The job of Quaestor didn't just give Caesar experience of helping to run an important part of the empire. With the job, came a seat in the Senate – for life. When Caesar came back to Rome after his year abroad, he was at last one of the most important men in the empire.

He married again. His new wife was Pompeia, the wealthy granddaughter of his former arch-enemy, Sulla. He now had contacts and friends on both sides of the Senate, although he remained a populare all his life. He also had a new source of money – his new wife's fortune.

Pompeia may have brought Caesar an enormous dowry (the money a bride gave to her husband on marriage) but the way Caesar spent it, no amount of money seemed to last long. Especially with the new job Caesar now got, the post of *aedile*.

BREAD AND CIRCUSES

One of the main jobs of an aedile was to organise the games and entertainments which filled the time of the vast mob of unemployed and underemployed people who filled the streets of Rome. It would be like being in charge of all television, radio and film-making today. For any rising Roman politician, but especially a popularis like Caesar, getting the job of one of the four aediles was crucial for building a reputation as a friend of the people and buying their votes.

Many entertainments which were very popular in ancient Rome we would think of as horrible today. Slaves and criminals were specially trained to fight each other to the death; these were the famous *gladiators*. The best gladiators became superstars and made fortunes – enough to buy their freedom and set up their own gladiator schools. Wild animals would be made to fight and kill each other, or be 'hunted' around the arena by teams of slaves.

Caesar spent vast amounts of borrowed money on the most amazing circuses and games that anyone had ever seen. He paid to have gladiators dressed in solid silver armour. And instead of the usual gladiator fights, he had one arena filled with water and staged a 'sea-battle' with the gladiators fighting each other from ships.

To impress his fellow senators, Caesar decorated his house with the most expensive works of art. He even built a huge country house, then as soon as it was finished he had it pulled down because he didn't like it after all.

Caesar was living the life of a multi-millionaire, but it was all a sham. Caesar was in more debt than he'd ever been in his life before. He owed so much money to so many people, that even he didn't know if he'd ever be able to pay it back again. Unless he got a really important a job – a job where he could start taking bribes instead of paying them out – Caesar was going to be in big trouble.

DON'T CALL HIM BALDY

According to his biographers, Caesar at this time was tall, slim and broad-faced. He had a high-pitched voice and was *very* proud of his appearance.

Unfortunately, he'd started going bald when he was only in his twenties and, being vain, tried to hide it by growing his hair long at the back and combing it forward to try and hide his bald patch. As Caesar got older, and even the hair at the back started to get thinner and thinner, this must have looked more and more silly. By the end of his life, he employed four personal barbers who would all work at the same time to arrange his hair to try and hide his baldness.

His political opponents used to make jokes about it, which Caesar hated... Suetonius, who wrote a book about Caesar, claimed: "Of all the honours voted him by the Senate and people, none pleased him so much as the privilege of wearing a laurel wreath on all occasions." I expect you can guess why.

But his vanity could make opponents underestimate Caesar. Cicero, one of his political enemies, admitted:

"When I notice how carefully arranged his hair is and when I watch him adjusting the parting with one finger, I cannot imagine that this man could conceive of such a wicked crime as to destroy the Roman Republic."

SMOOTH OPERATOR?

Strangely, for someone so obsessed with hair loss, Caesar used to have all his body hair plucked out with tweezers. *Ouch!* This would have been done while he bathed. Caesar, like many Romans, was very keen on taking baths.

Roman baths were not just a quick wash down in hot water. Romans took *hours* to bathe.

Roman baths were much more like what we would call saunas or Turkish baths, followed by a work-out in a gym or fitness centre.

Caesar's body hair.
retain for
possible re-use
on head.

The idea wasn't to wash yourself clean, but to sweat yourself clean, starting in a hot steam room called a *calderium* and then going on to a *really* hot room called a *sudatoria*. While you were sweating, a slave would scrape all the gunk and muck off your body with a special long-bladed knife called a *strigel*.

After the steaming and strigelling, you would plunge into a freezing cold pool called a *frigiderium*. And then, if you were still feeling grimy, you could do it all over again.

As well as cleaning yourself, there were masseurs to give you a massage if you felt a bit stiff and achey, and gym equipment like

weights and heavy lead-filled balls to lift to give yourself a work-out.

One of the things which made Caesar popular with ordinary Romans, were the baths he paid for. Not only did he pay for them to be built, but he also made sure that the price of admission was incredibly low. Thanks to Caesar, even the poorest Roman could afford to go to the baths and be boiled, frozen and have all his or her body hairs plucked out – just like Caesar himself.

Caesar had one major health problem. He suffered from epilepsy – fainting fits. Apart from that he was incredibly fit for most of his life. When he was a teenager, Caesar used to train every day at the Campus Martius. Here he and the other boys would practise sports like wrestling and discus throwing, that are still played today. They would also play a number of ball games, using balls like our modern footballs made of hexagonal pieces of leather sewn together and then blown up.

Even in his forties and early fifties, he was fitter than many of his troops who were half his age. He fought most of his battles on foot, in the front line of his troops. There are stories that if the army came to a river, Caesar would jump in and swim, or float across on animal skins, and he was often the first to get to the other side.

Chapter 7

WHAT NEXT?

Caesar still couldn't pay back the enormous debts he'd accumulated. Only one of the very top jobs, being one of the two consuls, could wipe out those kinds of debts, and maybe satisfy Caesar's ambition.

But although Caesar had done very well, he still didn't have enough influence or power to stand a chance of being elected consul. Getting to the top in Rome was very much like climbing a ladder. All the steps were already set out and you had to follow them one at a time. Just like a ladder, if you tried to miss out three rungs, and jump instead of climb, you could find yourself in a lot of trouble. Caesar could see, from the example that Pompey had set, exactly what he had to do next.

POMPEY

Pompey was
   the most famous and
   powerful general in the
   Roman army.
   This was how he did it...

Pompey's golden rules for being top general:

• **Always be on the winning side**

In the civil war, Pompey started as a Marius supporter, then changed sides when it became obvious that Sulla was going to win.

• **Know when to be loyal to the boss**

Sulla sent Pompey to fight the supporters of Marius who had fled to Sicily and North Africa. Many surrendered to Pompey, expecting their old friend to be merciful. They were wrong. Pompey executed them all. Pompey became known as 'Sulla's butcher'. Sulla was very grateful.

• **Know when to stand up to the boss**

Sulla wasn't grateful *enough*. Pompey wanted a triumph – a

victory parade through the streets of Rome – as a reward for defeating the supporters of Marius. Sulla refused, so Pompey marched his troops to Rome and camped outside the city walls until Sulla gave in.

Lesson that Caesar learned from Pompey:	Caesar's next goal:
• Leading an army means never having to say that you're sorry.	• To be a governor of an important province, and to command his own army.

BACK IN THE ARMY

Once again, Caesar got the job he wanted: governor of Spain. The only problem was, the moneylenders he owed money to wouldn't let him leave Rome. They believed that if they let Caesar leave Rome, they would never see their money again.

Caesar desperately started searching for someone – anyone – who could get him off the hook, and out of Rome. He found him.

Crassus was Rome's richest slum-landlord. As people from the provinces streamed into Rome looking for work or the dole, men like Crassus built high-rise blocks of flats, called *insulae*, to house them. Often, these insulae were so hurriedly and badly built that they fell down, killing everyone inside. Crassus had an unusual method for buying land and houses to rebuild. He would wait for a

fire to break out, then he would offer the owners of the burning house – and the owners of all the neighbouring houses – a knock-down price to sell their houses on the spot. At one time or another, it was said, Crassus had owned most of Rome.

He'd also commanded armies. In 72BC a slave revolt, led by a gladiator named Spartacus, had started in Capua and quickly spread to Rome. The Senate made Crassus commander-in-chief. He defeated Spartacus and then crucified 6,000 of the rebels along the sides of the main road from Rome to Capua, as a warning to any other slaves who might have been thinking of rebelling.

Crassus agreed to help Caesar now, if Caesar helped *him* in the future.

Crassus promised Caesar's creditors that whatever happened to Caesar, he (Crassus) would pay off at least a quarter of all the money Caesar owed. This was good enough for the moneylenders. Caesar was allowed to leave Rome to take up his new job.

Army life was the life that Caesar loved best. From boyhood he'd always enjoyed physical sports. Away from the soft life of Rome, Caesar's body got leaner and fitter and his mind got tougher.

Caesar knew that this was his big opportunity to become a really big shot. The Spanish legions, like the other legions of the Roman army, had no real loyalty to the city of Rome. Most of the legionnaires had never seen Rome; many had Spanish 'wives' and children (even though they weren't supposed to). And the oath of loyalty they took when they joined the Roman army was not to the empire or to the Senate but to the commander of their legion.

The only senators the soldiers trusted were their commanders, but only if those commanders gave them what they wanted – loot. And the only way to get loot was to have a good war against a weaker enemy.

Caesar did just what his soldiers wanted. As soon as he arrived in Spain he made sure the army was properly equipped and fighting fit, and then invaded Portugal. It was his chance to give his troops what they wanted (and a chance to grab some of the loot for himself too).

Caesar and his army marched across Portugal killing and stealing all the way. Even towns that surrendered were looted and burned.

At the end of his year as governor of Spain, Caesar had the loyalty of the Spanish legions, *and* he'd been awarded a triumph by the Senate in recognition of his victories.

TO TRIUMPH OR NOT TO TRIUMPH?

Caesar was a vain man, and a triumph was the greatest honour that could be given to a Roman general. It was a procession through the streets of Rome that officially declared: "This person is a hero". To a Roman it was like winning an Olympic gold medal, an Oscar and being interviewed on national television all rolled into one.

On the day of his triumph, the victorious general rode into Rome, at the head his troops, surrounded by cheering crowds. Behind the legions came a display of the loot they'd captured, laid

NEXT TRIUMPH
15 MINUTES

out on wagons and carts for the people of Rome to marvel at. Right at the end of the procession came the prisoners who had been captured and would be executed in public at the end of the triumph.

It was such a head-swelling experience that the rules said that a triumphant general had to have a slave riding in his chariot with him whose sole job was to whisper in the general's ear, "Remember – you are mortal!"

Caesar should have been delighted to be awarded a triumph, but he wasn't. Caesar had a big problem.

The rules of the triumph were very strict. A triumphant general was not allowed to come into the city until the day of the triumph itself. At any other time this would not have been a problem for Caesar, but just before the agreed date for Caesar's triumph, the elections for consul were to be held.

All the money Caesar had borrowed, all the crawling and flattering he'd done, all the battles he'd fought, had all been leading up to one thing – to be elected one of the two consuls of Rome.

Caesar knew he stood his best chance in these particular elections. He'd won the support of the people by providing wonderful shows; he'd won the support of the populare senators with bribes and promises; he'd won the loyalty of the Spanish legions; and now he was a great popular hero. Things would never be this good again.

But the rules of the election were as strict as the rules of the triumph. All candidates for election had to be present in the city during the election, and the election for consul was to be held *before* his triumph. What could Caesar do? If he accepted the triumph he couldn't stand for consul; if he entered the election for consul he would have to give up the triumph, the greatest day of any Roman's life.

After turning it over and over in his mind, Caesar decided to give up the triumph and enter the contest to become consul. He won.

Caesar was now the joint prime minister for a year – the most important man in Rome. (There was another consul, of course, a man named Bibulus, but when he left home to go to the Senate, Caesar's supporters threw dung at him! In the end, Bibulus just stayed home leaving Caesar to run everything.)

Surely now Caesar had everything he wanted, and could do anything he wanted.

NO.

TRIUMVIRATE

One of the best things about being consul happened at the end of the year, when you were given a province to rule.

But the Senate didn't want to give Caesar an important province to rule. Caesar was already too powerful for their liking. If Caesar became a ruler of an important province the senators all knew what he'd do – start a war, make lots of money from looting, and come back to Rome even more famous and even more powerful.

The Senate offered Caesar 'Italian woods and cattle tracks' to rule after his year as consul:

CAESAR : 0   SENATE : 1

Caesar was furious, but he didn't give up. He got Crassus to help him. They bribed and persuaded as many senators as they could. But they still didn't have enough power to get Caesar what he wanted:

CAESAR & CRASSUS : 1
SENATE : 1

Then Caesar did something brilliant. He added one more person to his alliance – Rome's most powerful general, Pompey.

Pompey: *While you're consul, will you give my retired soldiers land to live on?*

Caesar: *Always happy to help the army! And to show we're really good friends, you can marry my daughter Julia.*

Pompey joined the alliance with Caesar and Crassus, which became known as the *Triumvirate*, the Latin word meaning 'three rulers'.

CAESAR & CRASSUS & POMPEY : 2

SENATE : 1

Chapter 8

GAUL

With the help of Pompey and Crassus, Caesar ended up being governor of *three* provinces: the area to the east of Rome; Northern Italy; and, best of all from Caesar's point of view, southern Gaul (southern France). Caesar now had his own empire of more than 320,000 square kilometres to do what he liked with, and with a bonus – the Senate had been forced to make him Governor for five years, not the usual one.

Caesar was now ruler of southern Gaul, but most of Germany, Belgium, France and Switzerland was independent, although linked to Rome by treaties.

THE GALLIC WARS LASTED FOR SEVEN YEARS.

To make sure everyone heard of his exploits, Caesar recorded the whole war in a book he wrote: *De Bel Gallico* (On the Gallic War). He wrote it in the third person, speaking of himself as 'Caesar' and not 'I' and 'me', so it reads like another person's account of Caesar's victories. As you can probably guess, it's full of tales of Caesar's bravery, Caesar's cunning and Caesar's brilliance.

Caesar made no secret of the fact that entire tribes were slaughtered, towns and villages destroyed and whole populations enslaved.

> So ended the battle by which the tribe was almost annihilated and their name almost blotted out from the face of the earth...

Caesar decided to make an example of them...
he had all their councillors executed and the
rest of the population sold as slaves.

Caesar sold off an entire district of the town
in one lot. The dealers gave him a receipt for
53,000 people...

Caesar remained in their territory for a few
days, burning all the villages and cutting
down the crops...

Caesar decided to make an example of them
to deter the rest. He spared the lives of those
who had taken up arms against him, but cut
off their hands, a punishment intended to
demonstrate clearly the evil of their ways...

Caesar even reached Britain, leading two raids in 55BC and
54BC. But he was never out of touch with what was going on in
Rome. All through the Gallic Wars, Caesar often travelled to the
borders of Italy to meet either Pompey or Crassus. They did various
deals. For example, Pompey and Crassus made sure that Caesar

got an extension on his governorship. In return, Caesar sent some of his troops to Rome on leave so that they could vote for Pompey and Crassus in the next elections for consuls. Fairly unsurprisingly, the two of them were elected.

END OF THE TRIUMVIRATE

Although the arrangement between Caesar, Pompey and Crassus seemed to be working well, it didn't last.

SOL 54BC

Julia, wife of top politician Pompey and only daughter of Caesar, conquerer of Gaul, dies in childbirth.

Her husband was old enough to be her father! Did Caesar sell his daughter for support against the Senate?

Will Caesar and Pompey stay friends now they're no longer family?

AND TODAY in your sensational, soaraway Sol... Page III sensation Tiresias – is he for real???

TRAGIC DEATH OF POMPEY'S WIFE

Now he had no family tie to Caesar, the optimate senators started trying to persuade Pompey to turn against Caesar. Then Crassus was killed.

IN DIES LUDUS 53BC

Crassus killed in Asia Minor

CRASSUS' LATE SAVE

SPOT THE SPEAR...
mark with an X

TOP TRIUMVIRATE TERMINATED!

Millionaire builder and soldier skewered somewhere in Syria
– Ouch!

See back page for latest gladiator results

But Pompey was as ambitious and proud as Caesar. Pompey was used to being top general in Rome. Caesar's victories – which Pompey had helped bring about through his support – now threatened Pompey's own position.

In Dies Speculum 53BC

CLASH OF THE TITANS....
Caesar 7/3 .....
Pompey 2/1 ....
outsiders 100/1 ...

CAESAR AND POMPEY BATTLE TO BE BOSS

Allies on collision course: While Caesar stays in Gaul, optimate senators are busy trying to win over Pompey to the anti-Caesar camp. But Senate insiders say: "Beware of Pompey! Nothing less than being dictator will satisfy either Caesar or Pompey!"

The Senate saw its chance to disgrace Caesar. It drew up a list of charges against Caesar, crimes he was said to have committed while he was Consul. One of the crimes he was accused of was theft on a vast scale.

November 27th 51BC

In Dies Speculum

I CAME! I SAW! I BURGLED!

Optimates claim: "Caesar to blame"

real gold

Caesar's no fool gold

FAKE GOLD BAR SCANDAL ROCKS ROME!

As senators continue to investigate Caesar's crimes when he was Consul, way back in 59BC, it's been claimed that a number of gold bars in the state treasury have turned out to be bronze painted to look like gold. All fingers have pointed at Caesar.

Senators – including Pompey, Caesar's old ally – are demanding that Caesar comes back to Rome from his estates in southern Gaul to stand trial.

The Senators who opposed Caesar – most of them – demanded that Caesar come to Rome in order to stand trial. Pompey agreed.

Caesar absolutely refused to come to Rome. But the senators wanted to disgrace Caesar, nothing else would satisfy them. Every time Caesar suggested a compromise, the senators refused. Eventually, after months of arguing, Caesar marched his legions into Italy, crossing the boundary of the River Rubicon, to fight it out with Pompey and the senators.

IN DIES SPECULUM

Jan 11 49BC

CIVIL WAR!

With any luck we can keep this out of the history books.

CAESAR CROSSES THE RIVER RUBICON
SENATORS FLEE TO GREECE

Italian cities near the border with Gaul were today hurriedly building walls and ditches to try and keep out the legions of Caesar. Having seen what he did in Gaul, no-one's taking any chances! Worried citizens are asking: "Will Pompey protect us?"

Chapter 9

CIVIL WAR OR
WORLD WAR?

If you look up civil war in the dictionary, it will tell you it's a war fought within a country between groups of citizens from that country. But this civil war wasn't fought in just one country, it was fought across the whole Roman empire, between troops from almost every nation in the empire.

As Caesar marched his troops through Italy many people packed up and fled; they knew how Caesar had treated the Gauls! Most of the Senators fled to Greece. Some Italian towns built hasty defences – walls and ditches – to try and keep Caesar and his army out.

But as he marched through Italy, Caesar did something very clever. He *didn't* order his troops to burn the towns they captured, and he didn't have his opponents killed. He merely asked the people in the towns he captured to promise not to fight against him. Soon, many towns were welcoming Caesar as a hero.

Cicero, one of Caesar's most bitter opponents, complained:

"The country towns are treating him like a god... What honours these towns offer him! They are delighted with the cunning kindness of Caesar!"

Pompey went to Greece with his army; but he wasn't running away. Pompey knew that Caesar's army would have to get all its food and supplies sent all the way from Italy, because Greece was controlled by the senators who were Caesar's bitterest enemies. Pompey thought that if he forced Caesar's army to follow him to Greece, they'd run out of food and weapons *and* be outnumbered. Pompey was absolutely sure he could destroy Caesar.

The two great armies met at a place called Pharsalus. Caesar had 22,000 men, Pompey 45,000. The night before the battle, Pompey and his officers were so confident they'd win the battle they sat up most of the night arguing about how they would share all Caesar's wealth – who would get which of Caesar's villas; who would get his best farms and olive groves. They didn't think Caesar stood a chance. They were wrong.

Caesar was an expert on warfare. He'd carefully studied Pompey's usual tactics. Every time Pompey moved his infantry forward, Caesar's troops were there, waiting for him. It must have seemed to Pompey as if Caesar were a mind-reader. Whatever Pompey tried to do, Caesar anticipated him. Pompey's mighty army was destroyed – 15,000 of his men were killed and 24,000 were captured (more than Caesar's whole army!)

Pompey escaped, and fled to Egypt to try and raise a new army. Caesar chased after him. But when Caesar arrived at the Egyptian port of Alexandria, the Egyptian boy king, Ptolemy, sent him a special present – Pompey's head.

CARRYING ON WITH CLEO

Caesar stayed on in Egypt, fighting battles and falling in love with Cleopatra, Ptolemy's sister. When he finally returned to Rome in

46BC, he demanded – and got – four Triumphs. There was a whole month of celebrations, at the end of which Caesar was made dictator, for ten years, not the usual six months.

But after the celebrations came the reality of being in charge. Rome and the Empire was in a mess – much of it caused by Caesar and the civil war. Caesar was now the only real power in Rome, so he had to try and sort out the mess. The Senate still met, but no-one – least of all Caesar – paid any attention to its debates.

The first thing Caesar did was to reward his soldiers. As he'd promised, he gave his veterans land – land he'd confiscated from rich men who'd been on the losing side in the civil war. Then he rebuilt the ruined cities and created new towns of retired legionnaires in Greece and North Africa.

When he'd finished rewarding the army, Caesar started reorganising Roman life. He wrote new laws and developed a new calendar of 365 days with a leap year every four years. Helped by just a few friends – especially Mark Antony, who became Consul – Caesar worked from dawn till dusk. Sometimes, according to Suetonius, Caesar dictated four letters at a time to four different secretaries while at the same time reading complicated state papers!

FOOD FOR THOUGHT

For the first time in his life, Caesar started to suffer from long periods of bad health. He was working too hard, but he was also eating at far too many banquets.

The army food which Caesar had eaten as a young man was, even by our modern standards, a very well-balanced, healthy diet. The staple food was wheat, which the soldiers ground themselves and made into wholemeal porridge, bread or biscuits. This was eaten with vegetables, cheese, some fish, a little meat – usually bacon, olive oil and rough wine. In fact, on several occasions when the wheat ration was short and they had to eat more meat instead, the soldiers complained.

Roman breakfast (*frumentum*) and lunch (*prandium*) were also quite light and healthy meals. But the formal Roman banquets were becoming marathons of greed. Romans feasted lying down on three couches around a large square table. They didn't use knives and forks, but ate with their fingers (slaves came round after every course to wash the diners' hands). A Roman feast was a mixture of meal and cabaret, with jugglers, dancers and acrobats entertaining the guests between courses. And by the time Caesar became dictator, the food itself had to be part of the entertainment; hosts tried to devise more and more exotic, unusual (and often indigestible) dishes.

Petronius, a Roman writing after Caesar's death, describes a feast that included pastry eggs with songbirds in the 'yolks', and sows udders stewed in fish sauce. But the high point of the meal was when a pack of hunting dogs burst into the dining room followed by a group of slaves carrying a huge roast boar. When one of the slaves cut open the bulging belly of the boar, live thrushes flew out of it which were caught in nets by the other slaves and offered to the guests as appetisers before they ate the roast boar itself.

Like many wealthy Romans, Caesar loved feasting and was known to take emetics – potions like salt water to make himself sick – before a big meal so that he could eat even more. No wonder his health was poor if he was vomiting, then gorging himself, and then repeating the same thing the next day, and the day after that.

Chapter 10

THE FATAL MISTAKE

When Caesar was made dictator, he increased the number of senators from 600 to 900 so that he could reward some of his less politically powerful friends by making them senators. He also gave citizenship to non-Italians.

The changes to the Senate and to the laws of citizenship were too much for many of the old senators, especially the optimates. They were certain now that Caesar would never be satisfied until he'd destroyed the Republic and had himself made king. Caesar, in his determination to sort out Rome's problems ignored them, but the senators were not as powerless as he thought.

In February 44BC, Caesar made his fatal mistake – he had himself proclaimed *Dictator for Life*.

This was the last straw for the Senate, even for several senators who had previously been Caesar's supporters and friends. Trying to become king was a crime which was punishable by death. Although Caesar publicly refused a crown when Mark Antony offered it to him, Caesar was now a king in all but name.

A group of senators decided to take the law into their own hands. They knew that the only way to stop Caesar was to kill him; and they decided that it was their duty to do so.

Caesar was to attend a meeting of the Senate on 15th March – what the Romans called the 'Ides of March'. He'd been unwell and his wife, Calpurnia, pleaded with him not to go. She claimed to have had bad dreams – omens of death. Other strange signs had been seen foretelling doom. A fortune-teller had told Caesar that something bad would happen to him on the Ides of March. Caesar ignored them all.

The Senate was being rebuilt, to accommodate all the new senators, so the meeting of the Ides of March was to take place in the great stone theatre which had been built on the Campus Martius by Pompey.

Caesar pushed his way through the crowd gathered around the theatre. He saw the fortune-teller.

"The Ides of March are here," said Caesar.

"But not ended," replied the fortune-teller.

Caesar entered a long colonnade which led to the hall behind the stage where the Senate meeting was to take place. Before he could leave the colonnade, Caesar was surrounded by a group of 23 senators. Each produced a dagger and – as agreed – so that no-*one* would be to blame, they all stabbed. Most of the wounds were just scratches, and in the melee some senators cut each other, but one dagger plunged deep into Caesar's chest. Seeing his friend Brutus he groaned, "Not you too, Brutus!" Then, in shame at his weakness, or maybe in imitation of a priest at a sacrifice, Caesar pulled his toga over his head, slumped to the floor and died. Standing above him, like a witness to his destruction, was a marble statue of his old ally and murdered rival, Pompey.

OH YES,.... HIS LAST WORDS WERE 'ET TU BRUTUS'. MAKE SURE YOU GET THAT DOWN!

PRESS

Chapter 11

FRIENDS, ROMANS, COUNTRYMEN...

Many people today still believe that Caesar was the greatest of heroes; a strong man who was not afraid to start wars – even civil wars – to fulfil his ambition to make the Roman Empire even bigger, and to rule it alone. Kings, emperors and modern dictators have admired Caesar and taken him as an example to follow. Some rulers have even tried to suggest that they were in some way his direct descendents. For example, the words *tsar* (the title of the Russian emperors before 1917) and *Kaiser* (the German monarchs until 1918) are both versions of the name Caesar.

Others take the opposite view. One modern writer has calculated that around two million men, women and children died in the Gallic War. This would make Caesar one of the greatest mass-murderers and war criminals in history.

What can't be denied is that Caesar was one of the few men to almost single-handedly change the course of world history. If you try to imagine what would have happened if there had been no Julius Caesar you'll see what I mean.

Without Caesar the Empire might have fallen apart. He set the example of being a military dictator which the later emperors followed.

As the first emperors were Caesar's sucessors and members of his own family, without Caesar there would have been no Roman royal family and no emperors.

Without Caesar Gaul and Britain might not have been invaded, and Britain would not have become part of the Empire. Britain might have stayed a Celtic country of small tribes, and not been united under Rome.

Many British, European and American laws are Roman in origin, or follow the example of Roman laws. Even the calendar we now use is based on the one Caesar invented. We might have had none of these without Caesar.

Without Caesar's example to follow, there might have been no tsars or kaisers; no Napoleon and no Mussolini. And without those empires, there might have been no first or second World War.

Europe and the world might have been a much better place without Caesar and the Roman Empire, or it might have been worse: it would certainly have been very different.

If that sort of influence is what people mean when they describe Caesar as a "great man" they're probably right. But whether Caesar was a good man or a bad man... that's for you to decide for yourself.

Joan of Arc
and the burning
issues of the time
BAR-B-Q TONIGHT
BRING YOUR OWN STAKE

Chapter I

Go Get 'em, Girls!

For ten points... who is the greatest female fighting heroine the world has ever seen?

Think hard.

No, harder than that...

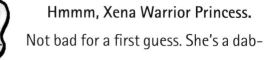

Hmmm, Xena Warrior Princess.
Not bad for a first guess. She's a dab-
hand with a broadsword, she can outdo
most men in the muscles department,
and she ALWAYS gets her own way. Not to
mention her magic powers, of course.

But not quite right, I'm afraid. No ten points.
You'll have to think again...

Okay, Buffy the Vampire Slayer. Now you're
getting warmer. Even if you're the world's
greatest Warrior Princess fan, you'd have to
admit that sweet little Buffy outdoes big bad
Xena every time. Even though Buffy's only
half Xena's size and strength, she
doesn't need the help of weapons.
She just wipes out her enemies with
her bare hands. With a toss of her
long, perfectly blow-dried, blonde
hair, she simply lets loose a few
carefully placed punches, adds a
somersault or two for good luck, and

then high-kicks her victims into little piles of dust. And the bad guys aren't human – oh no, that would be too easy. They're supernatural!

But sorry... still no ten points. Have another go.

TING! Correct. Take ten points and have a bonus five because I'm feeling generous... **Joan of Arc** (also known as 'Joan the Maid' or 'the Maid of Orléans' or 'St Joan') is the female fighting heroine to top all female fighting heroines.

For a start, our Joan was a real person, not just a made-up character on the TV. This is, of course, a major advantage in the scoring, and more than balances out the fact that 'Joan of Arc' isn't half as exotic or glamorous a name as 'Xena Warrior Princess' or 'Buffy the Vampire Slayer'.

Next, Joan was only 17 years old when she began her fighting career – even younger than Buffy. And she didn't just lead a gang of high school students; she

inspired whole troops of French soldiers, defeated the English army in several important victories, and was the main reason why an heir to the French throne finally won his crown.

Finally, when it comes to the old 'magic' rating, Joan beats Xena and Buffy hands down. Inexplicable things happened to Joan her whole life long. She insisted that she heard heavenly voices and saw visions. She made several predictions that came true. She is said to have had amazing healing abilities. She also knew the whereabouts of a lost, sacred weapon that some believed was magic. (The story of how she came to possess her strange, ancient sword is even more mysterious than the tale of how King Arthur came to own Excalibur.) Joan's strange powers were so extraordinary that she became famous far and wide – and many people became convinced that she was a witch...

There hasn't been a female fighting heroine like Joan of Arc since she was born over 500 years ago. Joan lived at a time when women were expected only to be housewives – whether you were a queen looking after your castle or a peasant looking after your hovel. So exactly how did a young village girl come to be the King of France's right-hand man (so to speak)? In the days before freedom fighters were even called freedom fighters, what did she do her freedom fighting for? And does her tale end happily, like all Xena and Buffy episodes?

If you want to find out more, read on for the inside story...

Chapter 2

Rowing Royals and Suffering Citizens

If you enjoy getting birthday cards and presents, stuffing your face with birthday cake, and playing mad birthday party games, thank your lucky stars you weren't born in medieval times. Birthdays were nowhere near as important then as they are now. Like many medieval people, Joan of Arc didn't even know exactly when hers was – although she thought she was probably born in 1412.

Now you might think that not having birthdays would make life pretty miserable. But I can assure you, in 14th- and early 15th-century France, that was the very least of the people's problems.

THE POPULATION TAKES A POUNDING

Between 1348 to 1350, the plague (also called the Black Death) swept across Europe inflicting a painful, messy death on hundreds of thousands of people. First, you'd have a headache and start throwing up. Then you'd shiver and sweat with a temperature. Big lumps the size of eggs would swell up in your neck, armpits and groin. Finally, gasping for breath, you'd turn purple and die. And you were extremely lucky if you escaped from it. According to a certain Henry Knighton:

There died in Avignon in one day 1,312 persons, according to a count made for the Pope... And the sheep and cattle wandered about through the fields and among the crops, and there was no one to go after them or to collect them. They perished in countless numbers everywhere, in secluded ditches and hedges, for lack of watching, since there was such a lack of serfs and servants, that no one knew what he should do... The living did not suffice to bury the dead.

Welcome to La Pierot. Population 3,157 1

So many people died throughout Europe that landowners found that peasants were suddenly in very short supply. This was good news for your average European peasant and bad news for your average European landowner (well, those who survived, anyway!) because the landowners were forced to offer the peasants much higher wages than usual to get them to work on their land. But on top of this, French landowners and peasants had other problems to deal with, too...

WAR... WAR... AND MORE WAR!

The French had been at war with the English for 11 years before the Black Death struck, and the plague did nothing to stop it. The troops went on marching, camping and battling on French soil year after year, decade after decade. Coupled with the devastating effects of the Black Death, this crippled the countryside. The few peasant farmers who were left struggled to grow enough crops and rear sufficient livestock to feed the landowning lords and their soldiers, let alone themselves and their families. Even worse, bands of *ecorcheurs*, or 'skinners' roamed the country. These unemployed mercenary soldiers and bandits plundered towns and villages, stealing everything of value and burning anything else. Worst of all, the war showed no signs of stopping. By the time our heroine Joan was born in 1412, the war had been raging on French soil for a whopping 75 years!

KEEPING IT IN THE FAMILY

The seeds of all the trouble were really sown way back in 1066, when the French Duke William of Normandy defeated King Harold at the

Battle of Hastings and claimed the English throne. (You remember the story – it was literally 'one in the eye' for poor old Harold.)

William the Conqueror (as he became known) drew England much closer to the Continent, particularly France. For instance, William gave much of England to the French lords who supported him. And French was even the language spoken at the English royal court for some years.

By the early 15th century, most of the French and English lords were closely related to each other. And they weren't any better behaved than families are today. They constantly bickered and fell out and fought amongst themselves – particularly over who was going to get all the money and property when a relative snuffed it. (And when I say 'fought', I really mean 'fought' – with armour and lances and swords.) When King Charles IV of France died in 1328, a huge family squabble broke out over who was going to get the French throne. Charles's cousin, Count Philip of Valois (who was French) and Charles's brother-in-law, King Edward III (of England), both claimed that they should be the next king of France. From a legal point of view, there wasn't much to choose between them. So Edward III wasn't at all happy when the Parlement of Paris decided that Philip should have the crown. In fact, Edward was so miffed, that in 1337, he went to war over it.

MADMEN, MALICIOUS MOTHERS, AND MAYHEM

The family squabble between the nobles turned into an international war between the English and the French that raged on for years – right into the next century. Year after year the fighting was fierce and bloody, but the French just managed to hold on to their crown. However, in the early 1400s, their fortunes began to take a turn for the worse. It began to look extremely likely that they would lose the throne to the English, for several reasons:

Reason 1

The Duke of Burgundy was the richest and most powerful of all the French lords. In 1407, he fell out with the Duke of Armagnac – another rich, powerful French lord (although not quite as rich and powerful as the Duke of Burgundy). As usual, the disagreeing dukes didn't just settle their differences with a scrap in the playground, they dragged their followers into it too. Their lands and armies were so big that this meant there was civil war within France. Now the French people were fighting each other, as well as the English.

Reason 2

The French king at the time, Charles VI, developed a mental illness and went totally mad. Everyone knew he could pop his clogs at any moment, leaving the throne up for grabs. The English heir at this time was King Henry V, who was bold and determined. He also had a huge army to back up his strong legal claim. Henry and his English forces had conquered a lot of French territory. He had even won the backing of some of the French nobles, including...

Reason 3

... the Duke of Burgundy (who, don't forget, was the richest and most powerful of all the French lords – a very good person to have on your side). This came about in 1416, when the Duke of Burgundy decided to side with his noble English relations across the Channel, rather than his French countrymen. (You've heard of the saying 'blood is thicker than water'?) The duke announced his support for Henry V and pledged that he and his Burgundian forces would fight for the English king. Together, the English and the Burgundians went on to occupy most of northern France – they even took Paris itself.

Reason 4

While the English claimant to the throne, Henry, was in a very strong position, the French claimant was in a very weak position. The French called their official heir the *Dauphin* (no, not the 'dolphin'), who was at this time the mad king's son, Charles. Well, at least the OFFICIAL position was that Charles was the mad king's son. In private, everyone had BIG doubts, because the queen had openly taken a lover – the mad king's brother, who was in fact much more likely to be Charles's dad than the mad king himself. This left big questions open over Charles's right to be Dauphin, and many of the snooty nobles in the French court looked down their noses at him. No one was 100 percent sure whether they should support him or not.

Reason 5

In 1419, Charles the Dauphin did something really stupid – he arranged the murder of the Duke of Burgundy (who, as you know, was fighting for Henry and the English). Firstly, this didn't do Charles any good, because the duke's son became the new Duke of Burgundy and took over just where his father had left off. Secondly, killing the richest and most powerful of all the French lords made Charles even more unpopular with the rest of the nobility. Worst of all, it REALLY annoyed his mother, the queen, because the Duke of Burgundy had been one of her best friends!

CHARLES' ROOM

I want you to tidy your room and stop murdering my friends

The queen paid her son back by agreeing to the Treaty of Troyes with the English. She signed away Charles's rights to the throne and agreed that on her mad husband's death, the French crown would DEFINITELY go to Henry V of England.

This was obviously a big kick in the teeth for Charles, and as you can imagine, he was extremely peeved. The few supporters the Dauphin still had left encouraged him not to take no for an answer. So Charles established a government-in-exile and tried to raise funds to pay for the French army to fight for him. Now, wars cost a lot of money, and after 83 years of fighting both sides were running short of cash. At one point, Charles was so skint that he had to sell the tapestries from his own walls to pay for his wedding! Even so, he managed to keep hold of some territories in southern France.

At last, in October 1422, the mad king died. King Henry V of England had died two months earlier, so after all that fighting he never got to be king of France anyway. But straight away, his baby son (another Henry) was proclaimed king instead – of both England AND France. As this was what had been legally agreed, no one publicly dared to argue with it – except for Charles the Dauphin, who stubbornly also declared himself king of France. So now France effectively had two kings – and the baby Henry VI held more territory than Charles did.

The French people themselves were split – they largely supported whoever held the territory in which they lived. So who knows how things might have turned out, if our Joan hadn't arrived on the scene to sort it out...

Chapter 3

The God Squad

Quick question: Joan of Arc never existed – true or false?

a) True.

b) False.

c) Sort of.

If you answered **c)**, have 25 points.

There definitely was never anyone called 'Joan of Arc'. Our heroine was called 'Jhennette' when she was born, though her family called her just plain 'Jhenne' or 'Jeanne' as she grew up. (Spellings weren't as important in those days as they are now.) 'Jeanne' translates into English as 'Joan'. The 'of Arc' bit of her name wasn't given to Joan until at least 50 years after her death. Historians and poets made it up from the French *d'Arc*, which is a fancy, aristocratic-sounding interpretation of her father's surname, Darc. But in fact, even though Joan's father was a man of some local importance, he was far from aristocratic – he was just the keeper of the village cattle-pound! And besides, his surname might not even have been Darc at all. In the documents that tell of Joan, his name appears as Jacques Tart, Tarc, Dare and Day – as well as Jacques Darc!

However, we know that our heroine was definitely a real person, because there are a handful of surviving historical documents which tell us about her. We have three letters that Joan herself dictated (she couldn't read or write); letters from other people written about her; references to Joan in other chronicles of the time; and the records of her eventual trial and the investigations into it that followed.

HOME, SWEET HOME

Joan was born and brought up in a little village called Domrémy, which was split in half by the Moselle River. The houses on the east bank of the river were in territory held by the allies of the English, the Burgundians. The houses on the west bank of the river (including Joan's) were in territory held by the French forces of Charles the Dauphin. As Joan grew up, she got used to seeing the local lads coming back from the river all bloody from fighting with the boys on the other side.

Well that showed them, didn't it?

Joan had to be careful not to venture too far into the fields when she was playing, for fear of bumping into marauding soldiers. So she spent a lot of time spinning and sewing at home with her mother, Isabelle – a very religious woman who inspired a deep love of God in her daughter.

POPE POWER

Joan's mother was a Catholic, because in medieval times, there weren't different Christian churches like the Church of England, the Baptists and the Methodists. All Christians were Catholics, and the Catholic church was (and still is today) told what to do by the Pope in Rome. Of course, the medieval kings and queens of Europe were Catholic too, so they also had to obey the Pope (often much to their annoyance). For instance, in 1095 Pope Urban II asked for the European royals to send knights to go to Jerusalem to throw out the Turkish rulers (who were Muslim). This started off a whole series of holy wars called the Crusades, which used up loads of the kings' time, money and best nobles (most of the knights were captured or killed by the Turks and never came back). King Richard the Lionheart of England was away so long on one Crusade that his subjects must have almost forgotten who he was...

In theory, the Pope was the most important person in Europe. Massive, magnificent stone cathedrals were built in the 12th and 13th centuries that rivalled and often bettered royal strongholds. And under the Pope, the Catholic church had the power to make laws and recommend that people were punished if they broke them. As Pope Boniface VIII wrote in 1302:

All this of course meant that kings and their laws came a definite second – which the kings often found to be a right royal pain. Archbishop Thomas à Becket reminded King Henry II of England about this in a letter in 1166. Becket wrote: '... it is certain that kings receive their power from the Church... so you have not the power to give rules to bishops'. Henry II was so cross that he had Becket promptly murdered in his own cathedral.

But even though the kings often got fed up about being ruled over by the Pope, they did get one benefit out of being part of the Catholic church – a pretty BIG benefit, in fact. Everyone believed that kings were appointed by God (the 'divine right of kings') and that they ruled with God's authority. Which made it very hard for anyone to criticize what they did.

This also made it even more confusing in early 15th century France to decide who should have the throne – the baby Henry VI or Charles the Dauphin.

Which is exactly why Joan of Arc was so important...

AM I SEEING THINGS?

One summer's day in 1425, when Joan was about 13 years old, she heard a voice and saw a light coming from the right-hand side of her village church. This was the first of many times Joan heard voices speaking to her, and she later saw visions of St Michael the

Archangel, St Catherine and St Margaret, too. The earliest message Joan heard was: 'Be a good girl and God will help you'. But as the months went on, the voices became more urgent. They told Joan that:

- She must go to the help of Charles the Dauphin.

- She should lead the Dauphin's forces in lifting the siege of the mighty city of Orléans.

- She should conduct Charles to a proper coronation at Rheims cathedral (where he would be anointed the true king with the special holy oil that was kept there).

- She should drive the English back to their own country.

Phew! Pretty daunting demands for a young, uneducated country girl. Yet Joan was convinced that the voices came from God and she should obey them. She had no doubt that God meant Charles the Dauphin, not Henry VI, to be the king of France.

SUPER-CELEBRITY SAINTS

Medieval people were into saints in a big way. Everyone who was anyone had to have a bit of a dead saint – called a relic. People boasted that they had saints' bones, teeth and hair; cloth from Our Lady's robe; wood from baby Jesus's manger – even the whole head of John the Baptist! Today, the most famous relic is a piece of material called the Turin Shroud – people have only just recently decided that Jesus's body couldn't have been wrapped in it. It was the same with medieval relics – no one could tell whether or not they were fakes (and of course, most of them were). But they were taken very seriously. People went to great lengths to get their hands on them – whether it was by stealing them or paying for them. And relics were such big business that there were plenty of fraudsters who had them on offer – after all, how was anyone to know that they were walking round with a pig bone instead of St Peter's kneecap?

Relics, lovely relics – John the Baptist's fingers, St James' pants..... a stone once trod on by St Andrew.

195

Some people today believe that if you only pray hard enough, certain saints can protect you or work particular miracles for you. But in medieval Europe, EVERYONE believed this. The best saints to put your money on were the Fourteen Holy Helpers, who were particularly popular from the 14ᵗʰ century onwards.

Now imagine you are a medieval French peasant (wearing your oldest, dirtiest, smelliest clothes might help with this). Can you match the following Holy Helpers to the list of favours that you might need to pray for on the opposite page?

1. St Barbara
2. St Blaise
3. St Christopher
4. St Cyriac
5. St Denis
6. St Erasmus
7. St Eustace
8. St George
9. St Giles
10. St Pantaleon
11. St Vitus

A. Help for mad people, people who had fits, and people who couldn't have babies.

B. Protection against lightning, fire and sudden death

C. Help for hunters.

D. Protection for travellers.

E. To cure fits.

F. To cure headaches and rabies (a type of illness you can catch from mad dogs).

G. Protection against demons and evil spirits.

H. To cure tuberculosis (a horrible type of chest infection).

I. To cure colic and cramp.

J. To cure sore throats.

K. Protection for soldiers.

Answers:

1. B 2. J 3. D 4. G 5. F 6. I 7. C 8. K 9. A 10. H 11. E

The remaining three Holy Helpers were St Achatius, who for some reason didn't have any particular job, and Joan's favourites: St Catherine and St Margaret.

According to tradition, St Catherine was a Christian who lived in Alexandria in the late 3rd century – which was very unlucky, because the then Emperor, Maxentius, ordered all Christians who lived in Alexandria to be killed. Catherine argued her case for believing in God so well that she convinced 50 judges (who Maxentius had put to death immediately for being foolish) and also won over Maxentius himself – who fell in love with her. When Catherine knocked him back, saying that she was in love with Christ, Maxentius didn't take it very well. He had Catherine tortured on a contraption of wheels and knives (from which the firework 'Catherine wheel' takes its name). Not content, he then had her beheaded.

In the 15th century, St Catherine was probably the best-loved saint of the day. She was the patron saint of philosophers and students – and of course, wheelwrights! She stood for independence and courage, and was an especial favourite for young, unmarried women – like Joan.

There are several versions of St Margaret's legend:

- She is said to have disguised herself as a man and lived in a monastery as a monk called Pelagius – until she was accused by another woman of being the father of her baby! Rather than revealing she was a woman, Margaret suffered in silence and was punished by living in solitary confinement on bread and water for the rest of her life. She only owned up to being a woman on her deathbed! (This wasn't as unusual as you may think. Several other female  saints disguised themselves as men and ran off to live in monasteries, such as St Euphrosyne, who died in 470 after living for 38 years as a monk called Smaragdus.)

- In another version of Margaret's story, she was swallowed by a dragon and then born again out of its belly, totally unharmed. This made her the patron saint of pregnant women.

- Margaret is also said to have seen visions of Satan. This made her a good saint for people to pray to if they wanted help for those possessed by the devil.

- Margaret was also meant to have been dead against marriage – literally, as it turned out, because like St Catherine, in yet another version of her story she was tortured and killed for her vow of singledom.

St Michael the Archangel was another favourite saint in Joan's day – especially with knights, as he was always shown with armour and a sword, having battled the devil and won. This warrior saint was particularly popular in France, and he had been the patron of soldiers from Normandy when they conquered England and during the Crusades. 'Michael' is 'Michel' in French, and the monastery in northern France called Mont St Michel was a favourite destination for pilgrims in the 14th and 15th centuries. Even mad King Charles VI

went there in 1394 in the hope of curing his madness, and because he got a little better for a while, he named his daughter 'Michelle' as a thankyou. Charles the Dauphin made St Michael even more trendy. When in 1419 the English got hold of an abbey named after St Denis, the patron saint of France, Charles gave St Denis the sack and had St Michael painted on his soldiers' standards instead!

Of course, there's no way of ever proving that Joan's voices really were saints speaking to her. But Joan certainly believed whole-heartedly that they were. Later on, you'll find out just how much she trusted in them...

Chapter 4

Tried and Tested

Joan's first problem was how on earth to get close to the Dauphin.
Joan knew that her father would be furious if she went off with
Charles's troops. Everyone viewed the women who rode pillion
behind soldiers as little more than prostitutes. In fact, Joan's father
once warned that he'd rather his three sons drowned his two
daughters than have the girls become camp followers. (Sounds like a
nice man!) So Joan ran away to stay with her older cousin, Durand
Laxart, and begged him to take her to the provincial governor,
Captain Robert de Baudricourt, in his mighty castle at Vaucouleurs.

Joan's first audience with de Baudricourt didn't exactly go very well. When the young peasant girl told the powerful captain that God wanted him to send her to the Dauphin, de Baudricourt simply told Laxart to send Joan back to her father with a smacked bottom! But Joan didn't give up. She tried again... and again... and even once set off on her own to see the Dauphin. (She turned back before she got very far because she decided that she wasn't going about things the way her voices wanted her to.)

While Joan was waiting for things to work out, her voices told her one day that the French had lost a very important battle for the city of Orléans. In turn, she told de Baudricourt of the defeat and warned him that if he hung about much longer, it would be too late.

After de Baudricourt found out that Joan's news was true, he seemed much more keen to send her to the Dauphin. (Surprise, surprise!) Mind you, he got a priest to check she wasn't possessed by the devil, first! Luckily, Joan passed the test. Finally, it was time to go!

WE'RE OFF TO SEE THE DAUPHIN...

Today, it's only old stick-in-the-mud fuddy-duddies who mind girls wearing trousers instead of skirts. And few people raise an eyebrow if they see a girl dressed as a boy or a boy dressed as a girl – it happens all the time on the Jerry Springer TV show! But in medieval times, if this sort of thing went on at all, it only ever went on behind closed doors. Medieval people thought that 'cross-dressing' was truly outrageous. In fact, it was a sin against church rules. Nevertheless, Joan decided that she would go and see the Dauphin dressed as a boy. Her voices told her to do it – and in any case, it was safer that way. The journey was going to be through territory swarming with dangerous bandits and soldiers who didn't exactly act like 'gentlemen' when they came across ladies. No one could argue with the common sense of Joan's disguise. So she borrowed some of her cousin's clothes and had her hair cut short and up over her ears, like a man. Little did Joan know at the time that this was going to get her into BIG trouble later on...

A SIGN OF THE TIMES

At last Joan arrived at the royal court at Chinon. And she soon found out that de Baudricourt's test was only the first of several tests she had to face...

Test number one

Joan had to convince the Dauphin that she really had come with God's blessing and that he really was God's chosen heir to the French throne. To do that, she needed to provide the Dauphin with a miraculous sign that could only be from God himself. To this day, no one knows exactly what this 'sign' was, but there are several theories:

- It's been said that the Dauphin tried to expose Joan as a fake by hiding behind his courtiers and putting someone else on his throne in his place. But this dastardly trick didn't fool the 17-year-old country girl. Even though she had never seen Charles before, she apparently turned away from the impostor, marched straight into the crowd, and knelt before the real Dauphin. For many people, this was proof enough that Joan was really receiving messages from God. However, other people still weren't convinced. After all, Charles was notoriously pot ugly. He was reported to have had a bulbous nose, a drooping lip, and to have been generally 'the ugliest man in Christendom'. With these kind of looks, surely it would have been hard to miss him!

- Other reports say that Joan prayed and a host of angels appeared, bringing the Dauphin a golden crown – a vision which it was said that 300 or so of the courtiers saw as well!

- Another theory has it that Joan had a private conversation with the Dauphin and told him that she knew all about a secret prayer he had made one night in his bedchamber. As the story goes, Charles had asked God that, if he wasn't the true son of the mad King Charles VI, he might be allowed to escape from France and live safely somewhere else. The fact that Joan knew all about this apparently got rid of all Charles's fears about his dodgy parentage and reassured him that he was the rightful king of France.

MAID OF HONOUR

Now Prince Naseem Hamed isn't a real prince, is he? And 'Posh Spice' isn't Victoria Beckham's real name either, is it? Many people change their names to help create an 'image' for themselves when they want to be publicly recognized and become famous. And Joan did just the same. When she introduced herself to the Dauphin, she called herself 'Jeanne la Pucelle', which translates into English as 'Joan the Virgin' or 'Joan the Maid'. It may be hard for us in the 21st century to understand why it would be important for anyone to be famous for not having a boyfriend. But for Joan, it was vital.

It's only over the past 100 years or so that people in the Western World have begun to see women as equally important to men. In fact, some people would argue that men are still thought in many ways to be better than women. But in medieval times, the situation for women was a million times worse than now. The medieval church actively taught that women's bodies were shameful and sinful. It spread the belief that it was by falling in love with women that men were dragged down into sin. Odo of Cluny wrote in the 12th century: 'To embrace a woman is to embrace a sack of manure'!

For this reason, women who didn't have boyfriends or husbands were thought to be pure and holy. Everyone believed that there was no way the devil could have anything to do with a woman who was a virgin. So Charles the Dauphin made Joan go for...

Test number two

Joan had to undergo a physical examination by Charles's mother-in-law and some of her ladies-in-waiting to check that Joan had never slept with a man. None of the women were trained medical people...

... but luckily, somehow, they were satisfied that Joan really was a 'maid'. For many people, the fact that Joan was as pure as Christ's mother, the Virgin Mary, was proof enough that her messages really were holy. Unluckily for poor Joan, Charles himself STILL wasn't quite 100 percent sure...

UNIVERSITY CHALLENGE

The Dauphin sent Joan to Poitiers, where he had gathered a university of learned theology and law professors, in an attempt to rival the English-controlled University of Paris. It was time for...

Test number three

For three whole weeks, the wise old men bombarded the 17-year-old country girl with questions about her background – particularly her voices, her visions, and her prophecies. Unfortunately, the records of Joan's examination at Poitiers no longer exist. However, we think that she made four predictions:

- The English would be defeated at Orléans and the besieged city rescued.

- Charles would be properly anointed king at Rheims cathedral.

- Paris would be taken back from the English.

- The Duke of Orléans would return from England.

The upshot of the examination must have been that the professors believed Joan was telling the truth. For at the end of it, Charles equipped Joan as a fully-fledged knight and sent her off to war!

Chapter 5

Arise, Sir Joan!

Joan was in fact never officially 'dubbed' or given a knight's title –
even though Charles later honoured her brothers, who appear to
have done nothing much at all, with the aristocratic name 'du Lys'.
(That's medieval justice for you!) However, the king did kit Joan out
with the full knight's regalia – an extremely expensive business!
Charles ended up paying for Joan to have:

A squire

All knights had to have their own squire. These were trainee knights who acted a bit like golf caddies do today – running around after their boss, fetching and carrying, cleaning and polishing, and generally being helpful. If you were lucky, and more importantly could afford to buy your own weapons, you one day got to be dubbed a proper knight yourself – then it was your turn to boss someone else about and you could get your own back. Joan's squire was a man called Jean d'Aulon, who remained faithful to her through thick and thin.

STANDARD

WAR HORSE

SQUIRE

PACK HORSE

LOADS OF MONEY

A suit of white armour

The very first knights had fought each other with lances and swords and worn chain mail for protection. But when the longbow was invented in the early 1200s, they found the arrows often went straight through – and who wants to look or feel like a pin-cushion? So safety-conscious knights started a new fashion – wearing 'plates' of armour over the most vulnerable parts of their bodies. By the mid-1300s, all canny knights ('canny' – get it?) were wearing whole suits of plate armour. These may have been incredibly uncomfortable (Joan slept in hers at first, to get used to it!) but at least knights stood more of a chance of staying alive.

Five warhorses and seven pack-ponies

Good horses were extremely expensive. But a knight didn't just need a brave, handsome horse to look the part at tournaments and win admiring sighs from all the ladies! A fearless, fast charger could mean the difference between life and death in battle. Sometimes horses were even taught to do their own fighting with their teeth and hooves. And a dead horse could always be fired over the walls of a castle on a catapult to attract lots of flies and germs into the enemy camp – hopefully also squashing some of the enemy as it landed!

A standard

All knights had their own family 'colours' or 'heraldry' – a design which told everybody at a glance who they were. (A bit like football team strips, really.) The designs were painted onto standards, or flags – and it was all very useful in battle. Firstly, all this marked out where your lot were, so you didn't end up attacking your mates. And secondly, it told the enemy whether it was worth keeping you alive or not – if you were from a rich family, you could be ransomed back for lots of money (as lots of knights were). Knights always chose pictures which they thought said a lot about them. Lions and dragons were always popular, although there were some very odd choices too – like porcupines and apples! Joan had a very fancy-schmancy standard. Her voices told her what to have on it: Christ holding the world between the angels Michael and Gabriel, above embroidered fleurs-de-lys (flowers which stood for France and the king) and the words 'Jesus Maria'.

Off-duty outfits

When Joan wasn't in her armour, she didn't dress in women's clothes. She still dressed like a man, in a hose and doublet, with a jaunty hat on her head. Her clothes were posh and expensive, made of cloth of gold and silk and fur. Fashions were very important to rich medieval people. Like celebrities today, nobles saw it as part of their job to show off how many lovely designer clothes they had. But in the 14th and 15th century fashions got very silly, as nobles tried to outdo each other. And it wasn't just ladies who wore over-the-top clothes – lords did it too! Everyone could put up with women wearing daft things – after all, they were women, they were meant to be foolish! But lots of people warned against men following fashions. Not only was it sinful to love luxury, but the lords' huge, heavy costumes made it very difficult to run away from enemies! Some of the silliest fashions were:

- Long, pointy 'winkle-picker' shoes. (Some were so long and pointy that a chain was fastened to the tip, so the wearer could hold them up when they walked to avoid tripping over!)

- Long, pointy sleeves. (Some dangled right down to the floor and must have got very dirty – nice!)

- Long, pointy men's gowns and women's skirts. (Some trains were so long and heavy that women needed pages to follow them around all day holding them up!)

- Long, pointy hats. (Queen Isabella of Bavaria had to have her doorways made higher because hers was so tall!)

THE SWORD UNDER THE STONE

The only thing that Charles didn't equip Joan with was a sword. He didn't need to – she had found one herself. Joan's voices had told her to send a messenger to a tiny chapel where supposed relics of

St Catherine were kept. As instructed, the messenger dug behind the altar – and discovered an ancient sword, obviously from the Crusades, that no one had any idea was there... Sends shivers down your spine, doesn't it? The tales of the girl-knight and her 'magic' sword certainly terrified the English!

NASTY KNIGHTS

When Joan found herself at last being taken seriously as a soldier, she must have been delighted. But don't get the wrong idea – not everyone was as happy about it. In fact, most of Charles's favourites were extremely UNhappy about the way the Dauphin was making a fool of himself by listening to an uneducated peasant girl. And most of Charles's main men were far from the chivalrous knights they should have been. In fact, Joan was right in the middle of a very motley crew...

- La Tremoille had been Charles's first advisor – until Joan came along and pushed him out of the way. So naturally, La Tremoille hated her right from the start. And he wasn't a man you'd want to have as your enemy. He had a reputation for murder, blackmail and highway robbery!

- Gilles de Rais was the original 'Bluebeard' of the fairytale – a ruthless cut-throat who was later hanged as an alleged sorcerer and mass murderer.

- Arthur, Duke of Richmond, (or 'Richemont', as the French called him) was an English man who went over to Charles's side when he failed to get a good job in the English army! He also had two of Charles's closest friends murdered – not that Charles seemed to mind too much!

- La Hire was a very good soldier, but a very bad knight. In fact, he was little more than a bandit. La Hire once went to stay with a lord in his castle, then threw his host into his own dungeon and refused to let him go until the lord gave him lots of gold, wine and a horse! All this of course went right against the 'fair-play' rules of chivalry...

So these were the type of men that little Joan found herself up against, when she was trying to make the Dauphin follow the advice of her voices. She had an enormous job on her hands, and the fact that the grim leaders of Charles's court listened to her at all shows just how amazing Joan must have been.

MAID TO MEASURE – GIRL SAYS SHE'S JUST THE JOB!

Joan had one big thing on her side – fame. From the minute Joan had first gone to see Robert de Baudricourt, news had begun to leak out that there was a young girl going around saying that she had been sent by God to fight for Charles the Dauphin. If they had had newspapers in those days, Joan would soon have been splattered across the front pages...

EXCLUSIVE

I KNOW JOAN'S NEXT-DOOR NEIGHBOUR'S TAILOR'S SECOND COUSIN! An in-depth article on the stunning young visionary!

You can imagine how the secret got out – one of de Baudricourt's servants probably told his wife, who told her sister, who told the

blacksmith's brother, who told his friends down the local tavern...
and before you could say "Prophets alive!", everyone was talking
about Joan and wanting to hear more about her.

FRENCH BRING OUT
SECRET WEAPON –
MAGICAL MAID
OF MYSTERY!

By the time Joan had seen Charles, 'miraculously' recognized him,
given him her heaven-sent predictions, and claimed her mysterious
sword – even the English troops had heard the gossip.

GIRL FROM GOD
PROMISES FRANCE
WILL BE FREE!
Faith in fortune teller grows daily

The French public acclaimed Joan as an amazing young visionary
who had been sent by the Lord and was going to save their war-torn
country...

HOLY OR A HOAX?

Although there are some people today who claim to hear heavenly voices and see visions, there aren't many. Most of those that do end up either being given their own ratings-winning TV show or being locked away in a mental hospital. As for those who say they believe in someone who professes to have strange powers, well – they're usually mocked for it. But back in medieval times, visionaries seemed to crop up much more often than they do now. Three of the most famous were:

- Elizabeth of Shonau (died in 1164), who had visions of the Virgin Mary and wrote essays warning women about the sinfulness of loving luxury.

- Hildegard of Bingen (died in 1178) – an accomplished scientist who also had heavenly visions from the age of five. She was later made a saint.

- Margery Kempe (born around 1373). She was a wife and mother who, after having visions and hearing voices, dedicated her life to God and took a vow never to sleep with her husband again.

As you can see, medieval people were used to their visionaries

being women. Then again, being a prophetess was probably just about the only way that medieval women could get their domineering men to listen to their ideas and opinions.

Whether the visionaries were female or male, medieval people took them much more seriously than people do today. In fact, you could say that visionaries were the medieval equivalent of Hollywood stars. For instance, in the early 15th century, when a visionary called Vincent Ferrer visited Lyon, so many people flocked to see him that they went to the trouble of knocking down a wall so everyone could get a clear view. Not even Leonardo di Caprio has had to have that done for his fans!

Luckily for Joan, the medieval French royals were particularly keen on consulting fortune-tellers (a bit like our very own royals Fergie, the Duchess of York and the late Princess Diana).

- Before Joan was born, King Charles VI regularly asked for the opinions of a prophetess called Marie d'Avignon, and his wife, Queen Isabella, kept a visionary called Marie de Maille at her beck and call.

- A visionary nun called Colette lived at the same time as Joan. After the mother of the Duke of Burgundy met Colette in 1406, she took her advice for the rest of her life.

- Before Joan came onto the scene, Charles the Dauphin consulted a famous visionary called the hermit of St Claude. The hermit gave him two predictions: firstly, that Henry V would soon die; and secondly, that Charles would have a son. (The hermit turned out to be right on both counts.)

- The French courtly tradition of believing in visionaries was so strong that it continued well after Joan's life. Charles's son, Louis XI, kept the holyman Denis the Carthusian at his court. And once when Louis was very ill, he summoned the hermit Fra Roberto of Calabria in the hope that the hermit could heal him.

ABRACADABRA!

However, being an ultra-fashionable prophetess wasn't the only reason why Joan became so popular with the public, so quickly. On top of that, the men and women of France were actually *expecting* a female visionary to appear and save them. There had long been a folk legend about a mysterious woman warrior who would one day put an end to France's troubles. No one knew quite where the idea had some from. Some people thought the prediction had first been made over 500 years ago by the famous monk Bede, or King Arthur's wizard, Merlin. But by the time Joan arrived on the scene, new rumours had revived the old prophecy. It was said that the prophetess Marie d'Avignon had had a recent vision that the female fighting heroine was about to show herself.

Sacré bleu...
A vision of
Joan having
a vision!

In the light of all this, even Charles's tough, thuggish advisors had to admit that perhaps Joan's arrival at court was meant to be. Still, they didn't like it much. And many of them made up their minds to keep her out of things as much as possible...

Chapter 6

Joan's Predictions Come True... Well, Some of Them, Anyway!

If TV had been around in Joan's day, news companies world-wide would have sent their top war reporters to cover the action. The French evening news might have sounded something like this...

28 April 1429

I am speaking to you LIVE from the French army camp outside the besieged city of Orléans. The soldiers have been sent to try and save the starving citizens locked inside. It's probably the most dangerous place in the whole of the country at the moment. The English already hold all of northern France, and if they manage to break this mighty stronghold, the gateway to southern France will be laid open for them as well. Surely the Dauphin couldn't survive such a defeat! As I speak, the English forces are on red alert in their garrisons, and reinforcements are on their way. There really isn't time for any arguing among the French commanders – but that's exactly what happened here earlier on today. The famous young visionary, Joan, was under the impression that the French forces would attack the English straight away. When the Duke of Alençon and Captain la Hire explained that the first priority was somehow to get relief supplies into the city, Joan was reportedly furious. People have told me she was even more angry when she realised that the advice of her voices had been ignored. Apparently Joan shouted, 'You KNEW my voices told us to go in from the north! So why are we approaching from the south?' I myself then witnessed one of the many miracles which seem to accompany this young girl wherever she goes. The French tried to set the supply boats afloat to sail them up the river and into the city, but the wind was set dead against them. Joan prayed for a while and all at once the wind totally changed direction. The boats sailed right into the city as if God himself was blowing into the sails. On that bombshell, it's back to the studio...

29 April 1429

*Here I am INSIDE the city of Orléans. Today has been an amazing day
for the French forces. Who would have believed last night that the
French soldiers would take just one day to enter a city that has been
besieged for more than six months! But everyone I have spoken to
here agrees that it was Joan and the wind change that made it
happen. Everyone saw the miracle yesterday, and from that moment
on, the mood in both camps completely changed. Here among the
French, the commanders stopped arguing and began to take Joan's
voices more seriously. The soldiers were inspired with new hope and
courage. They really believe that Joan has been sent by God and that
God will grant them victory. On the other hand, the English have*

obviously been terrified out of their wits by Joan and her amazing powers. This evening, when Joan led the French soldiers towards Orléans and right into the city, the English didn't even make a move to stop them. Joan has literally 'put the fear of God' into the enemies of France...

ARE YOU THERE JOAN? THE BATTLE'S UNDER WAY!

4 May 1429

Several important garrisons defending Orléans remain to be taken from the English. However, there was an important French victory today, here at the Fort St Loup. Once again, it was all due to the amazing young girl the English are now calling a witch – Joan the Maid. According to Joan's squire, she took a rest in the afternoon with strict instructions to the other French commanders to wake her if they decided to attack. Once again, the captains overruled the Maid and let her sleep on. When several French regiments had gone into battle and the fighting was well underway, Joan suddenly sprang up from her sleep, crying, 'My voices have told me they have gone to attack the English!' Apparently, she was in such a hurry to put her armour on and dash outside that she forgot her standard, and her squire had to pass it out to her through the window. The Maid made it to the battlefield just in time to save the French from defeat at the hands of English reinforcements. It seems that whenever the young country girl-turned-knight is on the battlefield, the French can do no wrong.

7 May 1429

Today I am outside the garrison Les Tourelles, with Joan's priest, Father Jean Pasquerel. Father, can you tell us about the Maid's latest prediction, please?

"Well, yesterday evening a very worried Joan told me that she was going to be wounded by an arrow in the chest."

Thank you, Father. Viewers, I can confirm that in the fighting today, Joan was indeed wounded by an arrow in the chest. I myself saw it happen. The injury would have prevented an ordinary knight from taking any further part in the fighting. But I can tell you that after a few prayers, the Maid was up again, inspiring the French and petrifying the English with her astounding recovery. Furthermore, as the English captain Glasdale was trying to retreat over the bridge, it collapsed under him. He and all his soldiers fell into the moat and were drowned. All the talk in the English camp tonight is of how the 'witch' Joan healed herself by magic and used her powers to deliberately collapse the bridge. However, nothing can dampen the French high spirits. They are more convinced than ever that the Maid is an agent of God.

8 May 1429

Tonight, the sound you can hear in the background is the ringing of church bells – a noise that has not been heard in Orléans since the start of the siege nearly seven months ago. For today, the French have finally won control of the city from the English! Joan now has approval at the highest levels of French society. The Archbishop of Embrun told me earlier that 'God has chosen a little flea to work for him and alight on the dunghill of France.' Now I'm off to join in the celebrations and it's back to the studio...

12 June 1429

You can see behind me the town of Jargeau, where today another English-occupied fortress fell into the hands of the French. However, as usual, the main talk tonight is not of the continuing French

victories but of the Maid, Joan. Today, she was struggling up a siege ladder while bravely carrying her standard, when an English soldier threw a rock that struck her hard on the head. It knocked her right off the siege ladder and sent her tumbling into the ditch far below. Joan lay motionless for several minutes, and the news spread like wildfire that she was dead. However, no sooner had the English started to celebrate than Joan was up on her feet shouting, 'Forward! Forward! God says the town is ours!' The English were so startled at the reappearance of the girl they call 'the witch' that they completely went to pieces. Every last English soldier was killed...

18 June 1429

Yet another of the Maid's predictions came true here today, at Patay. According to my sources, the Duke of Alençon asked Joan for her voices' advice on how the French should attack. Joan told him to 'use his spurs'. At first, everyone thought the Maid meant that the French should give up and gallop away. However, she corrected their mistake with a laugh and told everyone that by the end of the day, they'd be chasing the English as they fled. I can confirm that it all happened exactly as Joan said...

July 1429

Joan and her forces have now arrived here, in Troyes. Before the townspeople had met the Maid for themselves, some of them had begun to believe the English rumours about Joan being a witch. I have with me Brother Richard, who was sent out by the authorities to greet Joan and check whether or not she was good or evil. Brother Richard, can you tell me in your own words what happened, please?

"Well, having heard all about the Maid and her strange powers, I was extremely nervous about meeting her, I can tell you. I went out prepared with buckets of holy water and my best large cross, all ready to drive the devil out of her. However, Joan didn't seem at all bothered by the fact that I suspected she might be a witch. She just laughed and said, 'Don't worry, I won't fly off!' Rather embarrassing for me really. Actually, except for dressing like a man and praying rather a lot, Joan seems to me to be perfectly normal."

Thank you, Brother Richard. And I have some EXCLUSIVE news for our viewers tonight. Sources very close to Joan have told me that she has never killed a single soul. She acts fearlessly in battle, leading assaults on the enemy and carrying her standard into the thick of the fighting. However, she has never laid a hand on a single soldier and often weeps at the sight of the injured and dying – the English as well as the French. Viewers, we'll of course keep you updated with any new details about this extraordinary young prophetess just as soon as we have any...

17 July 1429

Today was the day that most people thought would never come. Charles the Dauphin was anointed with holy oil and crowned King of France here at Rheims Cathedral. Joan the Maid was at his side with

her standard – she said it had seen the suffering, so it was only right that it should see the glory too. Experts have noted that two of the prophecies Joan made to the university panel at Poitiers have now come true. Tonight, everyone is asking themselves whether it's only a matter of time before the remaining two prophecies come true, too. Joan the Maid is the talk of France...

August 1429

Joan-mania has hit an all-time high. The public is flocking to see her wherever she goes. They bring her sick babies to cure, and try to kiss her feet, touch her rings and rip off bits of her clothes as relics. The men and women of France are literally expecting miracles. They are making medals with Joan's face on and putting her picture up in churches, and generally treating the Maid like a living saint. Things are getting quite out of control. Some priests disapprove of it all very strongly. Even Joan herself doesn't like it! She refuses to attempt to cure people and tries to keep out of the limelight as much as possible. On top of all this bother, sources close to the Maid have told me that she is very frustrated by the new king's lack of action. Now Charles has been crowned, he doesn't seem to want to bother to order any further fighting. And as Joan has so often been heard to say, 'God helps those who help themselves'...

8 September 1429

At last Joan was today back in action on the battlefield, trying to take Paris back from the English. It was the first time the French forces had tried to take a major enemy stronghold since Charles's coronation. But today the tide of the war seems to have turned. The Maid and her army have today tasted the bitterness of a shock defeat. Tonight the English are rejoicing and the French are horrorstruck. Joan's critics are gloating, saying that the witch's magic has finally failed. They have pointed out that Joan shouldn't have chosen Our Lady's birthday on which to mount a major attack. Joan herself has refused to say that God has let her down. Instead, she has put the failure down to her own impatience. The Maid has let it be known that she went ahead without the approval of her voices, so it was her own mistake...

November 1429

There have been reports of many prophetesses in France since Joan first became famous, and today the Maid came face to face with one of them – a woman called Catherine de la Rochelle. Catherine told Joan that a white lady dressed in gold appeared to her every night and told her to travel through France trying to raise funds for the army – which is just what Joan herself is doing at the moment. Joan wanted to see Catherine's vision for herself. After all, the Maid's own visions are so real that she actually touches them. And on just two occasions,

it has been rumoured that other people have shared her visions with her. So the Maid stayed awake all night with Catherine – and didn't see a thing, even though Catherine insisted that the white lady came. Catherine was none too pleased that Joan didn't believe her story...

April 1430

Joan recently caused quite a stir when she prayed inside this very church for a baby that had stopped breathing and looked as black as death. The Maid's prayers brought it back to life just long enough for it to be baptised, so even though it died again, it could at least be buried in holy ground. However, I have to report that not everyone approves of Joan. Last week, the Maid did a deal to swap an English prisoner of war, Francquet Arras, for a French prisoner of war. However, today she found out that the French prisoner of war had died, so there was no one to swap Arras with. As Arras was a confessed murderer, the Maid had him executed instead. Immediately, some critics have accused the Maid of going against the code of chivalry by executing a prisoner she had already agreed to ransom. Controversy surrounds the Maid and is growing day by day...

23 May 1430

Today has been a disastrous day for the French. The unthinkable has happened. Joan the Maid has been captured! The French were attacking Compiègne, and while Joan was leading a brave charge, a Burgundian archer got close enough to her to grab hold of her cloak and drag her off her horse. I have been talking to the devastated French soldiers and can report that some of them think she was betrayed by her own people. They have told me that they think Joan was deliberately abandoned to the enemy by La Tremoille – after all, La Tremoille was King Charles's chief adviser until Joan came along

and he has reportedly always been extremely jealous of her. Some of the French soldiers I have interviewed reckon that La Tremoille ordered one of his henchmen to lock Joan and her troops outside the castle when most of the French had already retreated safely inside. I have been unable to find out whether this accusation is true or not. However, one thing is for certain: the country girl's courtly clothes were certainly part of the reason why she has come a cropper!

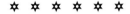

Chapter 7

A Dirty Dungeon and a Dismal Death

Whether you were a prisoner of war or just a plain criminal, it wasn't pleasant being a captive in medieval times. For a start, dungeons were damp, freezing, stinking, rat-infested stone pits – often without a single window to let in any light and little drainage to let out the sewage. Worst of all were 'oubliettes' – tiny holes deep underground into which the worst prisoners were thrown and just forgotten about.

Then there was torture. You could be stretched out on a machine called the 'rack' until your tendons snapped and your bones popped out of their sockets. You could have your thumbs squashed in thumbscrews, or your foot crushed in a contraption called the 'boot'. You could have your tongue ripped out of your mouth by a vicious iron tongue-twister. You could be hung from the ceiling in iron clamps – either around your wrists, or worse, around your feet, so you were left dangling upside down! And the torturers had many more ideas up their sleeves...

Worst of all, medieval people were so into cruel punishments that if you were put on trial, you didn't stand much of a chance of being found not guilty – even if you really WERE innocent!

A CLOSE SHAVE AND A NARROW SQUEAK

With Joan's reputation for magic, her guards must have been expecting her to disappear into thin air at any minute – which is in fact, what she very nearly did! As a special prisoner, they held her in solitary confinement. Joan was first kept in the tower of a château, with guards posted outside her room. In the middle of the night, the determined girl managed to remove enough of the planks in the floor to slip down silently into the unlocked room beneath. She got as far as the main entrance before the night patrol noticed her and raised the alarm!

After that, Joan was held in another tower. She very nearly vanished from that, too! Joan jumped out of a window in an attempt to escape. It was a very long way down – 18 metres, to be precise. She didn't exactly make a good landing either – those who found her thought she was dead. But once again, it didn't take her long to make a miraculous recovery.

OUT OF THE FRYING PAN, INTO THE FIRE

In November 1430, a deal was done to hand Joan over to her worst enemies – the English, who clapped her in irons and locked her into a cell in Rouen with the roughest soldiers they could find to 'guard' her (more like torment and harrass her). By the way, I hope you've noticed by now that the ungrateful Charles the Dauphin hadn't made a single attempt to rescue Joan, or even made an offer to ransom her – which was nearly always done, and for far lesser knights than Joan.

Unfortunately, the Catholic church had gradually become more and more suspicious about Joan's voices, visions and so-called 'miracles'. An official church court assembled (called the Inquisition), and over 170 judges began to question Joan to find out if they could charge her with the crimes of being a witch and a heretic (someone who refused to submit to the authority of the church). In those days they could arrest you, interrogate you and torture you first, with a view to charging you later – which was again bad luck if you hadn't in fact done anything wrong.

HUBBLE, BUBBLE, TOIL AND TROUBLE

The Inquisition wanted to give Joan as many bad marks as possible and ultimately find her guilty. There were several reasons why...

- The English hated Joan. They felt she had single-handedly turned the tide of the war against them and caused them to lose several important cities – not to mention hundreds of troops. **Ten out of ten bad marks for this one.**

- The church representatives were extremely niggled by the way Joan wore male clothes – and such fine, luxurious ones, too. They accused her of 'having cast aside all womanly decency'. But what niggled the grand, educated churchmen even more was that the simple peasant girl refused to do what they said and put a dress back on. Well, they couldn't be having teenage rebels going around defying the church, could they? Firstly, it made Joan a heretic. And secondly, it made them look very stupid. **So ten out of ten bad marks for that, too.**

- Medieval people lived in terror of those who were in league with the devil – witches and sorcerers who practised black magic. When a suspected devil-worshipper died, people cut off their right hand in the belief that this would undo the spells they had cast. And it wasn't just your average medieval peasant who thought this way. In 1326 Pope John XXII confirmed everyone's fears when he gave the church the official power to seek out witches and sorcerers and get rid of them. Only 63 years after Joan's death,

witch-hunting had become such big business that
two church Inquisitors wrote a book of
instructions (called the *Malleus
Maleficarum*) on how to do it properly as
a full-time career! Joan was in trouble
because the English had from the very
start declared that her strange powers
weren't from God – they were witchcraft.
(After all, Joan wasn't on their side, was
she?) The especially bad news for Joan was

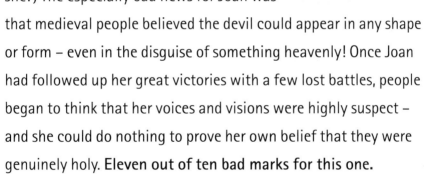

that medieval people believed the devil could appear in any shape
or form – even in the disguise of something heavenly! Once Joan
had followed up her great victories with a few lost battles, people
began to think that her voices and visions were highly suspect –
and she could do nothing to prove her own belief that they were
genuinely holy. **Eleven out of ten bad marks for this one.**

THE END IS NIGH

After four months solid of intense, hostile questioning, the
Inquisition found Joan guilty as charged. On the threat of torture
they ordered her to recant, which means going back on your word
and saying you've made everything up. The church firstly wanted

Joan to say that she didn't believe her voices and visions came from God after all. And secondly, that she'd do what they wanted and wear women's clothes. (She'd always insisted that she couldn't, because God had told her that he wanted her to dress like a man.) It seems that, for fear of being burnt alive, poor Joan admitted to all the church's accusations. However, some people say she was tricked into signing a confession – remember, she couldn't read, and she can't have been feeling on top form after all that time in an enemy prison, either.

By recanting, Joan had escaped burning. But she was horrified at the sentence that was meted out to her instead. She was ordered to put on women's clothing and condemned to be kept in solitary confinement for the rest of her life – and not even in a church prison, as was usual in this sort of case, but in a normal English prison. Within four days, Joan had changed her mind. She put on her men's clothing again and vowed that everything she had ever said was true. Moreover, Joan announced that her voices said she had greatly displeased God by saying that they had never existed. On 30 May 1431, Joan was led out to be burnt at the stake.

AN EVENTFUL EXECUTION

Joan never gave up her belief in God and that she had done what he wanted. And for some reason, her captors showed her some mercy and allowed her to see a priest for a last Mass – which they hadn't done all the time she was in prison. (This was especially strange because the church didn't allow recognised sinners to take Holy Communion.) While the flames licked around her body and the smoke curled upwards, Joan cried out repeatedly to Jesus, Mary and the saints. She asked for a crucifix and an Englishman hurried to make her one out of a few scraps of wood and held it up on a pole so she could see it. It took a long time for Joan to die, because the fire had been specially prepared to give her a slow, painful death.

There were several reports of strange things that happened when Joan died:

- One of the executioners is thought to have seen a white dove flying up out of the flames. Apparently he said: 'I greatly fear that I am damned, for I have burnt a holy woman.'

- Another person said that he saw the word 'Jesus' written in the flames.

- Several said that Joan's heart never burned away – even though sulphur and oil were poured on the fire in an attempt to set it alight.

Lastly, Joan's ashes were finally thrown into the river – firstly, so they couldn't be buried on holy ground, and secondly, so that no one could use her relics either in holy rituals or black magic. And that was an end to the matter... or so the Inquisition thought.

Chapter 8

Sorry! We made a mistake

Just like Elvis, Joan had become a legend in her own lifetime. In an age when there was no e-mail, telephone, TV, radio, newspapers or postal service – and when most people couldn't read or write anyway – Joan grew to be famous far and wide in a very short space of time (she was in the public eye for no more than three years). She was gossiped about on both sides of the English Channel by thousands of people who had never met her, as well as those who had. So many rumours went flying around about her that people were fascinated by her – even though they found it hard to know what was the truth and what was exaggerated or even totally made-up. Everyone wasn't going to forget about Joan that easily!

Some people were keen to believe that Joan was still alive – so keen that rumours soon went round that someone else had been burned at the stake in her place! These were made worse by the fact that false 'Joans' started to pop up all over the place, in an attempt to cash in on her fame.

Those who were more sensible and realised that Joan really was dead, straight away began to feel rather guilty and wonder whether she had been innocent after all.

- In 1450, when Charles had recaptured Paris and was well on his way to driving out the English (just as Joan had predicted), he opened a half-hearted enquiry into his heroine's trial.

- In 1452, even the church itself wondered whether it might have done the wrong thing and ruled that Joan's case should be re-opened.

- A proper investigation took place between 1455 and 1456 and the verdict of 'guilty' was overturned. Justice at last! But a bit late for poor Joan...

- In 1920, the Catholic church made Joan a saint. (Mind you, it took them long enough to get round to it!)

Today, Joan is admired as one of the national heroes of France – and after all that, rightly so, wouldn't you think?

Timeline

1412   Joan of Arc is born.

1422   August – Henry V of England dies. His son, Henry, is proclaimed king of England and France. Charles the Dauphin also proclaims himself king of France.

1422   October – Mad King Charles VI of France dies.

1425   13-year-old Joan sees her first vision in her village church at Domrémy.

1429   Joan travels to see Charles the Dauphin at the royal court of Chinon. Charles sets tests for her, which she passes, and she is then fully-equipped as a knight.

1429   April to July – Siege of Orléans. Joan leads French army in successful defence of the city.

1429   July 17th – Charles the Dauphin anointed as king of France at Rheims cathedral.

1429   September 8th – Joan loses battle trying to take back Paris from the English.

1430   Joan continues to see visions and use her powers of healing.

1430   April – Controversy surrounding Joan and her powers grows. Some see her as a witch.

1430   May 23rd – French attack Compiègne. Joan is captured.

1430   November – Deal is done to hand over Joan to the English. She is imprisoned in Rouen.

1431   Spring – Joan is tried and found guilty.

1431   May 30th – Joan of Arc is burnt at the stake.

1450   Charles now opens an enquiry into Joan's trial.

1452   The Church orders Joan's case to be re-opened.

1456   Investigation into trial – 'guilty' verdict is overturned.

1920   Catholic Church makes Joan a saint.

Chapter 1

Boney'll Get You!

I once met a very old man, who told me that when he was a very young boy his grandmother used to tell him that if he didn't go to sleep, or eat his greens, or do as he was told: "Boney'll get you!"

This "Boney" she threatened him with, this bogey man which used to terrify him, (and which she was probably terrified with as a young girl), was Napoleon Bonaparte.

Nowadays Napoleon isn't some monster used to scare children, but most British people still don't know much about the real Napoleon Bonaparte.

Here are some ideas about Napoleon:

He was very short.

Not true: he was 5'6½" (172 cm) tall – average for a Frenchman of his time. The rumour that he was only 5'2" (158 cm) comes from a mistranslation of the old French measurements which were different to the British ones.

 He was a ruthless dictator who only cared about personal
power, a tyrant like Hitler or Stalin.

Not true: he tried to bring fair laws and equal rights to the people of
France and the Empire.

 He once said: "Not tonight, Josephine!"

Not true: that line "Not tonight, Josephine" came from a
popular English comic song of the early twentieth century.

 He died of arsenic poisoning.

Not true: at least as far as the autopsy results are concerned.
When his body was examined, a large tumour – a cancer – was
found in his stomach. His father also died of stomach cancer.

The following account is about the real Napoleon, not the bogey-man.

An Island For Sale

Europe at the end of the eighteenth century, when Napoleon was born, was not made up of the nation states we know today. For example, there was no Italy, no Germany, no Belgium, no Hungary, no Czech or Slovak republics.

Most of Europe and the Middle East was ruled by three huge Empires: the Austrian (or Holy Roman) Empire; the Russian Empire and the Turkish (or Ottoman) Empire.

Italy was mostly divided between the Austrian Empire and the Pope, who was not just a religious leader but also one of the richest and most powerful princes in Europe. A few Italian cities were tiny countries in their own right. All the people spoke the Italian language, but there was no single country called Italy.

Napoleon's parents, Carlo and Letizia Bonaparte, were Italians living on the Mediterranean island of Corsica. Until just before Napoleon's birth, Corsica was ruled from the Italian town of Genoa. Napoleon's father, Carlo, was a nobleman, a lawyer and a fighter for Corsican independence.

Carlo Bonaparte was a friend and supporter of a Corsican rebel leader called Pasquale Paoli. Together they raised an army of Corsican rebels to fight the Genoese. Eventually, the Genoese decided to leave Corsica because of all the trouble caused by the rebel fighters.

This was what Paoli and Carlo had been hoping for. But they assumed the Genoese would just leave and let them run the whole island. The Genoese did not. This is what they did...

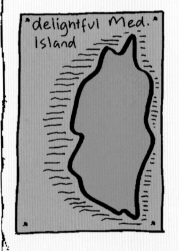

For Sale

delightful Med. Island

Delightful Mediterranean Island

Complete with olive groves, fishing ports and peasant farms.

Excellent opportunities for boar and partridge shooting. Plenty of pine trees and chestnut trees. All mod. cons. including mountains, cold running water and rebel fighters. Would suit large European nation with plenty of soldiers. One Careful Owner.

APPLY: GENOA

They sold Corsica to the King of France.

Free Corsica!

In 1768, the year before Napoleon was born, the French king took over his new island. Over the next two years, more than 30,000 French soldiers were stationed in Corsica. The Corsican rebels fought bravely, but they were outnumbered by French troops. Paoli, Carlo Bonaparte and the rebel army eventually surrendered to the French.

The rebels signed a peace treaty with the French. Paoli was allowed to leave the island to live in exile in England. He tried to persuade Carlo and his family to come with him. But Carlo had one baby son, Joseph, and his wife Letizia was pregnant with another child. Carlo and Letizia decided to stay in Corsica. Later that year Napoleon was born, a French citizen because Corsica was now part of France.

 But if Carlo had gone with Paoli, then Napoleon – France's greatest general – would have been born English.

Napoleon's Childhood

Although he was born a French citizen, for the first ten years of his life Napoleon didn't speak or write a single word of French. Like all the other children on the island he was brought up speaking and writing Italian.

Carlo hoped that his sons would

become lawyers. But education cost a lot of money, and money was something that Carlo and Letizia didn't have.

Then a friend told them about a special scholarship scheme run by the French government to pay for the education of the children of hard-up nobles – which was what Carlo and Letizia were. The only problem was that there were only two types of education offered under the scholarship: to train to become either a priest or a soldier.

It was too good an opportunity to miss, but should their two boys be priests or soldiers? Carlo and Letizia talked it over. Joseph was clever, dreamy and gentle. He wouldn't be much good as a soldier, but he might make an excellent priest.

But what about Napoleon? He was quick and clever, which a good priest should be. But he was also tough, proud and stubborn. Even though he was younger and smaller than Joseph, Napoleon would always beat him if the two boys fought. Although it would mean sending the boys to different schools, Carlo and Letizia decided that Napoleon would have to be trained to be a soldier.

So, in December 1778, Napoleon and Joseph, accompanied by Carlo, boarded the boat for France.

Carlo took the boys to a small town in southern France called Autun. Here they would learn French at the local school before going their separate ways – Joseph to the seminary to learn to be a priest, and Napoleon to the military school in Brienne. On New Year's Day 1779, Carlo said good-bye to the boys and caught the boat back to Corsica.

Napoleon's Schooldays

The military school in Brienne which Napoleon went to was a strict school. The boys wore army-style uniforms and slept in little wooden cubicles which were locked at night (they did have chamber pots in their cubicles, just in case).

Although it was a military school, all the teachers were monks. The boys were taught all the things that army officers would need to know such as maths, geography (especially map-making), and how to build fortifications.

They were also taught to be very patriotic. The monks taught the boys that France was the greatest country in the world, with the bravest army and the wisest king. The monks were so concerned to make the boys love their country that they sometimes told lies (not something monks are supposed to do). For example, in history lessons the boys were taught that:

 Germany had once been part of the French Empire.

 In the battles of Agincourt and Crécy the army of the French king had been defeated by French rebels (NOT the English army).

 France had never – repeat NEVER – lost a battle to the English.

The days in the school were very long indeed. This is the actual timetable for a typical day at the school when Napoleon was a pupil:

6.00 am Sleeping cubicles unlocked and cadets woken. Cadets wash and put on uniform.

6.30 am Class has early morning "pep" talk – similar to a class assembly – usually on French law and the importance of good behaviour.

7.00 am Mass.

7.30 am Breakfast: bread, fruit and a glass of water.

8.00–10.00 am Lessons in the usual school subjects: Latin, history, geography, maths and physics.

10.00–12.00 am Lessons in military subjects: how to build fortifications, drawing and colouring maps.

12.00 am Lunch (main meal of the day): soup, boiled meat, another meat or fish dish, dessert, and a glass of red wine mixed with water.

1.00 pm Recreation.

2.00–4.00 pm More lessons in Latin, history, geography etc.

4.00–6.00 pm Lessons in either fencing, dancing, gymnastics, music or a foreign language (either German or English) depending on the day.

6.00–8.00 pm Homework.

8.00 pm Supper: roast, a second meat or fish dish, and a salad.

9.00–10.00 pm Recreation.

10.00 pm Evening prayers and lights out.

Napoleon stayed at the military school for five years. This is his school report for his last year:

> He is very regular in his conduct and has always distinguished himself by his interest in mathematics. He has a sound knowledge of history and geography. He is very poor at dancing and drawing. He will make an excellent sailor.

What isn't mentioned in the report is Napoleon's worst subject: spelling. It was awful – probably because he hadn't learnt French until he was nearly ten years old. For the rest of his life, Napoleon misspelt even very simple French words and often mispronounced them too.

What might come as a surprise, though, is the last sentence of the report. At this time, the boy who would grow up to be France's greatest general wanted to be a naval officer.

Napoleon wrote a letter asking to join the navy. Possibly the letter got lost or maybe no-one bothered to reply, but when he got no answer Napoleon applied to the Military Academy in Paris to be trained as an artillery officer. This time he was accepted.

Chapter 2

The Rich Get Rich and the Poor Get Nothing

Napoleon had been brought up to believe that France was the greatest country in the world, with the best king and the bravest army. Coming to Paris was a great shock for Napoleon, because it was obvious that there were some big problems in France; problems which the monks had never mentioned.

What's that horrible smell of perfume?

The nobles – the rich lords and ladies – and the royal family lived in incredible luxury, while the poorest people starved in the streets.

Unlike Britain, France was ruled under the old, medieval feudal system. This meant that all the land was owned by rich nobles – lords, dukes and counts. Poor farmers – the peasants – had to pay the rich lords to farm the land. There were no elections in France and no parliament to make laws. The law was simply what the king said. He was an absolute monarch which meant that he had the absolute right to do whatever he liked.

One of the powers the king had was to send anyone to prison without trial just by writing a *lettre de cachet* – which means a sealed letter. It was a single sheet of paper signed by the king and sealed with wax. The person whose name appeared on the paper would go to prison or be sent into exile for as long as the king wanted. Louis XVI, who was king when Napoleon was a young man, signed over 14,000 *lettres de cachet* during his reign.

Lettre de Cachet

Go to Jail! Go directly to Jail and don't argue! You won't get a trial, and you'll stay there until I say you can come out.

Signed,

Louis (King)

PS. I don't actually know who you are or anything about you, but one of my ministers said you were bad, dangerous and deserved to be locked up and that's good enough for me.

On their own lands, the nobles had similar powers to a king. French peasants were virtually slaves to the lords who owned the land. Every year the peasants had to give part of their crops to their lord. They also had to work for no money building roads and bridges. French peasants had few possessions and hardly any money; the rich lords owned nearly everything.

There were some the things that the peasants had to do by law and there were some things lords *could* do by law. Work out which ones are True or False.

Peasants had to:
- work for free for the lord for several days every year
- pay a tax to their lord every year
- give part of their crops to their lord every year
- grind their wheat in their lord's mill and pay for using it
- bake their bread in an oven owned by their lord and pay for using it
- crush their grapes in their lord's press and pay for using it
- pay a tax on anything they took to sell at a market held on the lord's land

Lords could:
- ride across peasants' fields when hunting, even if there were crops growing
- keep rabbits, which the peasants weren't allowed to kill even if they were eating their crops

- keep pigeons, which the peasants weren't allowed to kill even if they were eating their crops
- ...but, because of all their privileges, the rich lords paid more taxes than the peasants

Every one of those statements is true, except for the last one. Believe it or not it, was the peasants – the people with hardly any money – who paid the highest taxes.

And not only did they pay taxes to the king, they also had to give one-tenth of all their income or the crops they grew to the church.

Got any spare change?

All the senior churchmen, such as the bishops and the cardinals, came from the wealthiest families. Like the nobles, the rich clergy also paid virtually no taxes.

You don't have to be a financial genius to work out that any country that depends for its money on taxing people with hardly any money is heading for disaster.

Revolution!

By 1789, Napoleon had left the military academy and was an artillery officer in the small garrison town of Valence in the south of France. French officers in those days were allowed to choose where they served, and Napoleon chose Valence because it was the closest garrison to Corsica. His father had died, and although he wasn't the oldest, the rest of the family looked to Napoleon to take over from Carlo as head of the family.

Napoleon and Joseph now had six younger brothers or sisters who all needed educating, clothing and feeding. Food was getting more and more expensive. Napoleon did his best help. He sent as much of his pay as he could home to his mother to help pay for the large family, but Napoleon's mother was struggling.

But families poorer than the Bonapartes were facing real hunger. In the summer of the year before, freak hailstorms had badly damaged the crops before they were harvested. Then the winter had been the worst anyone could remember – rivers and lakes had frozen for months. When the thaw came, the roads had flooded. What little food had been saved from the hail and ice couldn't get into the towns because of the floods. The price of bread rocketed. The poor people in cities such as Paris began to starve.

For years the ordinary people – the workers in the town as well as the peasants in the countryside – had been angry about the large amount of taxes they had to pay compared to the tiny amounts paid by the rich nobles. They were angry too about the privileges of the nobles, and they were angry about the *lettres de cachet*. The shortage of food was the final straw.

In the summer of 1789 the people of France turned to violence to get what they wanted. In Paris, an angry mob destroyed the Bastille prison, and in the country gangs of starving peasants attacked and burnt the houses of their rich landlords, often with the rich landlords still inside.

King Louis tried to control the growing revolution. He summoned the ancient French council – the Estates General – to meet at the Royal Palace of Versailles to suggest reforms. The Estates General renamed themselves the National Assembly and tried to become a proper parliament and rule France like the British parliament ruled Britain – passing laws to abolish the old feudal rights of the nobles.

But changes didn't come quickly enough for the poorest people in Paris.

In October, a crowd of women demanding bread, marched from Paris to the Royal Palace at Versailles. When she heard what they wanted, Queen Marie Antoinette was supposed to have said:

"If they have no bread, then let them eat cake!"

But she didn't say this. It had been said, but by Queen Marie Thérèse, the wife of Louis XIV, a hundred years earlier.

A riotous crowd broke into the palace, and forced the king and queen to come back to Paris and live in the Tuileries Palace instead of Versailles. The revolution was getting beyond the control of the politicians in the National Assembly.

Napoleon the Revolutionary

Far away from Paris, in the garrison town of Valence, news reached Napoleon and the other soldiers of the revolution in Paris.

Napoleon, the son of a freedom fighter, was an enthusiastic supporter of the Revolution. Although his parents had been nobles, Napoleon believed passionately in the principles of the Revolution: *Liberté, Egalité, Fraternité* – Freedom, Equality and Brotherhood. That meant: freedom for the ordinary people from unjust taxes and the feudal payments to lords; equality for everyone – the same laws for all; all Frenchmen are brothers – no more divisions into nobles and peasants.

Napoleon organised a club of pro-revolutionaries – a sort of political supporters' club. When the order came to confiscate church land and sell it to the ordinary farmers, Napoleon organised the sale in Valence.

Then in June 1791, the king did something very stupid: he tried to make a run for it.

Louis XVI had pretended to support the revolution, but secretly he'd been hoping that the revolution would collapse and the old ways could come back. Now he saw that wasn't going to happen, he and his family disguised themselves, slipped out of an unguarded door of the Tuileries Palace in the middle of the night, and drove by coach to the Belgian border. The coach was stopped at the town of Varennes, the royal family was recognised and brought back to Paris as prisoners.

Back in Valence, Napoleon made a speech publicly condemning the king's action.

Napoleon realised that many of the most senior officers in the army were still loyal to the king. Along with a number of other junior officers, he campaigned for the creation of a new army, a citizens' army: the National Guard.

In the autumn of 1791, Napoleon was rewarded for his support of the Revolution. He was elected as one of four lieutenant colonels of the Corsican National Guard. He was 22 years old.

War Against the Revolution

In March 1792, the old Austrian Emperor, Leopold, died. The new Emperor Francis II, was Queen Marie Antoinette's nephew, and was determined to destroy the French Revolution and rescue his aunt. He and the King of Prussia publicly promised to help Louis and Marie Antoinette. They also called on the other kings of Europe to join them.

The French army attacked first, but the Austrian and Prussian armies were much better organised and equipped. There were rumours, probably true, that Marie Antoinette sent some of the secret battle plans of the French army to her nephew, who shared them with the Prussians.

The National Assembly gave weapons to all the citizens of Paris so that they could defend themselves. The Prussian army came within a few miles of Paris before being beaten by the French army.

The Paris mob, which was now armed, turned on the king and royal family. Helped by the National Guard, they attacked the Tuileries Palace, killed the king's bodyguard of 600 Swiss soldiers, and took the royal family to the Temple Prison.

Chapter 3

The King Must Die

In September 1792 France was declared a republic – a state without a king. In November the ex-king Louis XVI was tried for High Treason and found guilty. In January 1793 he was executed by guillotine in Paris.

His personal servant stayed with Louis in prison to look after him. This is what he wrote about the day of his master's execution in his diary:

January 1793

I remained alone in the room, numb with grief. The drums and the trumpets announced that His Majesty had left the prison. An hour later, salvoes of artillery and cries of Long Live The Nation! and Long Live The Republic filled the air. The best of kings was no more!

The execution of the King of France horrified the other monarchs of Europe. Soon Austria and Prussia were joined by Britain, Spain and the Kingdom of Piedmont, in Northern Italy, in their war against France.

The French government set up an emergency committee, called the Committee for Public Safety, which had the power to do anything the 12 members thought necessary to save the Revolution from its enemies.

But although the Committee was popular in Paris, in the west of France thousands of peasants and supporters of the king began an armed rebellion against the government.

It was a revolution against the revolution.

The Reign of Terror

The Committee for Public Safety, led by a lawyer named Maximilien Robespierre, attempted to put down the revolt by executing everyone it thought was an enemy of the Republic.

A law was passed called The Law of Suspects. Under this law every town was to make lists of people thought to be against the government. In a single year a quarter of a million people were arrested and nearly 18,000 people were executed. In Paris more than 3,000 people were executed, including the queen.

That year was known as the Reign of Terror.

All the executions were carried out in public, in front of large crowds which often booed and threw rotting rubbish at the condemned prisoners as they were driven to the scaffold on open carts called tumbrels.

The Guillotine

It would have been impossible to execute so many people if it hadn't been for the guillotine. It was invented by a Dr Joseph-Ignace Guillotin who tested his new invention on dead bodies in the hospital at Bicetre. Dr Guillotin kindly offered the machine to the French Republic as the official means of execution. Unlike a man with an axe, he assured the committee, it could chop off heads all day and never get tired.

But even the guillotine couldn't execute people fast enough for the authorities in the west of France where the rebellion was strongest. 2,000 captured rebels were executed by being drowned in the river Loire, and in Lyons prisoners were lined up in front of mass graves and shot with cannons.

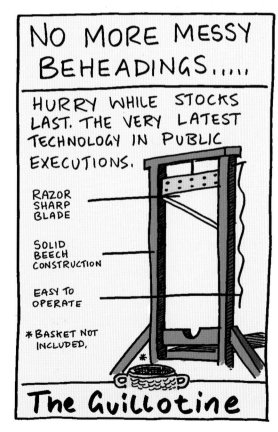

NO MORE MESSY BEHEADINGS.....

HURRY WHILE STOCKS LAST. THE VERY LATEST TECHNOLOGY IN PUBLIC EXECUTIONS.

RAZOR SHARP BLADE

SOLID BEECH CONSTRUCTION

EASY TO OPERATE

*BASKET NOT INCLUDED.

The Guillotine

Napoleon Saves the Revolution

The port of Toulon, in the south of France, was one of the centres of rebellion against the revolution. In August of 1793, the rebel leaders in Toulon declared the dead king's son to be the new king, Louis XVII, and they allowed a fleet of English, Spanish and Italian ships to come into the port and land troops there.

This was very bad news for the government in Paris. They already had more than 800,000 soldiers fighting against the armies of Prussia and Austria. They didn't have the men or weapons to fight another war in the south. This looked like it could be the end of the Revolution.

Just when things started to look really bad Lieutenant Colonel Napoleon Bonaparte volunteered to help fight the invading troops and the rebels in Toulon.

When he arrived, the town was under siege – surrounded by troops loyal to the revolution, but no-one seemed to know what to do next. Because of the shortage of good generals, the army surrounding the town was commanded by a former royal portrait painter, who was then replaced by an ex-dentist who got sick at the sight of blood. The siege was getting nowhere.

Napoleon took control. He led an attack on one of the forts defending the town, and from there organised an artillery attack on the British ships anchored in the port. Faced with a ferocious attack by cannons, the British admiral got the troops back on board and slipped out of port during the night.

But Napoleon had been wounded in the leg leading the attack on the fort. At first, the army doctor wanted to cut off his leg – this was the normal treatment for bad wounds, to stop them getting infected. After another examination, though, he decided to risk not amputating, so Napoleon was left with a deep scar, but two legs.

Napoleon Saves the Revolution Again

Napoleon was the hero of Toulon. As a reward for his services, he was promoted to Brigadier General at the age of only 22. He was also a friend of Augustin Robespierre, brother of the powerful leader of the Committee for Public Safety, Maximilien. Everything seemed be going Napoleon's way.

But no-one in France was safe from accusation, imprisonment and execution. Eventually, having denounced, imprisoned or executed nearly everyone who disagreed with them, the members of the Committee for Public Safety turned on each other. Robespierre himself was executed, with 71 of his closest followers including his brother, Augustin. As a close friend of Augustin, Napoleon was also imprisoned.

Fortunately for Napoleon, the people and the government had had enough of bloodshed. The Committee for Public Safety was disbanded and a new government was formed consisting of a council led by five ministers called Directors.

Napoleon was let out of prison, but no-one in the new government wanted to give him a job. He waited in Paris for a new post. He waited, and he waited. Although his pay should have been enough to live on, Napoleon was still sending most of his money to his mother, and Paris was the most expensive place to live in the whole of

France. When he ran out of money, Napoleon sold his carriage, and moved out of his flat to live in a cheap hotel. He couldn't afford a new uniform when his old one started to wear out, and had to walk around Paris looking like a tramp. He even gave up wearing gloves as (he said) "a useless expense."

Then one night, Napoleon decided as a rare treat to cheer himself up that he'd go to see a play – in one of the cheapest seats, of course. Walking to the theatre, he saw some National Guardsmen shouting anti-government slogans and gathering together an armed mob.

Napoleon went at once to the parliament building. Some representatives were panicking, and nobody seemed to know what to do. Napoleon offered to help.

Once again he used artillery guns, this time to defend the French government from a rebellion by the Paris mob. Once again he won, and once again he was a hero.

In Command

This time Napoleon got the reward he thought he deserved. He was put in command of the Army of the Alps. His job was to beat the Austrian army and their allies in Northern Italy.

Like many soldiers about to go to war, Napoleon quickly married his sweetheart, a widow with two children whose first husband had been executed during the Terror.

On March 9th, 1796, General Napoleon Bonaparte married Josephine Beauharnais, and two days later, on March 11th, he took up his new command. And all through the coming war, whenever there was a break in the fighting, Napoleon would take out a small framed picture of Josephine which he carried everywhere with him, show it to anyone who was nearby, and then tell them what a wonderful wife Josephine was. Then he would kiss the picture passionately and put it back in his pocket.

An Army of Scarecrows

You would imagine that Napoleon would have a crack team of highly-trained soldiers to defeat the might of the Austrians. If Napoleon had the same thought he was in for a shock. The army with which Napoleon was supposed to beat the Austrians in Italy was described by one of his fellow officers as "an army of scarecrows". That was far too complimentary.

None of the soldiers had real uniforms. Some of the older soldiers were still wearing the rags that were all that was left from their pre-revolutionary uniforms. Most wore whatever clothes they owned. Only a few had proper boots, and most of the soldiers either tied rags round their feet or wore homemade flip-flops made from plaited straw. They hadn't been paid for months and hadn't eaten in days.

Napoleon had been given a little money to pay for the war. He spent it all in the first few days. He bought 18,000 pairs of boots and enough corn to make three months supply of bread – but only if the soldiers mixed their flour with ground chestnuts.

But worse than the state of their boots or their rations were their weapons. They were old-fashioned to the point of being useless. The best equipped soldiers had old-fashioned muskets. These were the same sort the French army had been using for over a hundred years. Gunpowder and shot had to be poured down the barrel and pushed in with a ramrod. A soldier might be able to fire two rounds a minute, if he was a crack shot. But after about 20 minutes, he would have to stop – in the middle of a battle – and clean his musket.

But there was nothing Napoleon could do about the muskets. The army would just have to make do. If they won – and it was a big if – it wouldn't be because of their equipment; they would have to use what little they had very cleverly. It would take a lot of luck and some very cunning tactics.

Chapter 4

A Gentlemanly Occupation

The old rules of war, like the old rules of government, came from the Middle Ages. They were based on the old chivalric idea that war was a game for gentlemen, and no-one got hurt – except the peasant foot-soldiers, and they didn't count.

Most battles until Napoleon's time went like this:

 Two armies marched towards each other until they reached a place where both agreed they would have a battle – this was often done by the opposing commanders meeting each other for a friendly chat a day or two before the battle.

 Both armies got ready – sharpened their swords etc. This could take some time.

They faced each other on flat ground.

 They lined up in two long straight lines.

When everyone was ready they marched towards each other – in step.

 They fought for a few hours.

 Both sides went back to their tents.

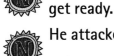 Result: usually a draw.

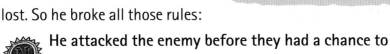

If Napoleon had fought by the old rules he would have lost. So he broke all those rules:

 He attacked the enemy before they had a chance to get ready.

 He attacked anywhere – not just on flat ground.

 He attacked from any direction – from the front, from the sides, from the back.

 He didn't give a fig for what was "gentlemanly" – he attacked where the enemy looked weakest.

He moved his troops incredibly quickly – attacking, winning, marching on again, then attacking again.

He insisted on discipline in his army – he did his best to stop his soldiers looting (stealing from civilians).

He demanded and got sole command of his army – he didn't like sharing.

Napoleon and his army of scarecrows thrashed the Austrian army – to the delight of the ordinary Italian people. They were delighted because not only did Napoleon drive out the Austrians from the north of Italy, but he also set up a new republic in the north of Italy based on the French Republic. That meant the old feudal rights of the nobles were abolished and there was a new fairer system of laws and taxes.

To Egypt

The Directors were so pleased with Napoleon's success in Italy that they promoted him again. He was made commander of the army to invade Britain.

Napoleon went to the channel coast to look at his troops. He was very keen to start the invasion as soon as possible, but what he saw made him call the invasion off. Most of the troops were badly-equipped young recruits, the

weather in the channel was appalling – gales and driving rain – and the boats for the invasion were poorly-built and leaky. If they tried to cross the channel, the British navy would easily destroy any ship that wasn't already sinking. Napoleon decided on another way to attack Britain – by going east.

Much of Britain's wealth depended on trade with the East, and in particular bringing to Europe crops and goods from India, which had recently become part of the British Empire. Napoleon decided to invade Egypt, which was part of the Turkish Empire. Then, if the invasion of Egypt was successful, he could march even further East – maybe even attack India itself.

Everything went well for Napoleon to start with. The French quickly defeated the Turkish army in a great battle fought near the pyramids. (Some people say that it was a French gunner in that battle who accidentally blew the nose off the Sphinx.)

But Napoleon hadn't come to Egypt just to fight. He'd also come to explore and learn. He brought with him scientists and scholars as well as soldiers.

Cracking a Code

Like many Europeans of the time, Napoleon was fascinated by the remains of ancient Egypt – the pyramids, the temples, the paintings and sculptures, and especially the strange picture writing or hieroglyphics. At that time, no-one knew how to read hieroglyphics. One of the scientists, a man named Tancret, made a great discovery.

He found a black stone near a town called Rosetta which had three different types of writing on it. One text was in ancient Greek, one in modern Egyptian and the third was in hieroglyphics. Tancret realised that the texts in modern Egyptian and ancient Greek were the same. So the hieroglyphics were almost certainly the same. He found, by comparing the three pieces of writing, that he could make out a name: Ptolemy. The texts were the same!

La Poste en Dimanche

BIG SET-BACK FOR REVOLUTION: Western France in Rebel Hands

What had been discovered was the key to the hieroglyphic code. It was a triumph for all the historians and scientists.

But the military side of the expedition had turned into a disaster. All the ships that had brought Napoleon's army to Egypt were anchored offshore near an Egyptian port called Aboukir. A British fleet commanded by Nelson found the French ships, surrounded them and sunk them. Napoleon's army was now stranded. They couldn't get back to France; they couldn't reach India.

For a year, Napoleon and his army were stuck in Egypt. They defeated the Turkish army again and set up a French-style republic for the Egyptian people to rule themselves. Then, in the summer of 1799, four French ships got through. On board one of the ships was a packet of two-week old French newspapers. Eagerly, Napoleon started to read the news from home.

The news was terrible.

Le Télégraphe

FRANCE AT WAR WITH BRITAIN, AUSTRIA, PRUSSIA, TURKEY & SICILY – and losing!

LA SOLEIL

La Soleil says:

Dump the dodgy Directors!

See page 3 for exclusive pics of Marie Antoinette, painted before she died!

Bring Back The king!

Long Live Louis XVIII!

Napoleon had saved the republic twice before. He was certain that he was the only person who could save it now. He took the four ships, and with a few friends and senior officers, returned at once to France leaving the rest of his army still stranded in Egypt.

It took another two years before Napoleon could arrange to get what was left of his Egyptian army back to France.

I'm in Charge

When Napoleon returned to France in 1799 he found things were as bad as the newspapers said. Napoleon at once organised a conspiracy to seize power, helped by his brother Lucien, who was already one of the five Directors.

The brothers went to the government council and told the

deputies that rebels were about to attack and capture Paris. The only way to stop the rebels, the brothers said, was to put Napoleon – who had already saved the Revolution twice – in charge of all the troops in Paris. They also said that it was much too dangerous for the council to stay in Paris, they should go somewhere safer. **All this was a complete lie.**

morning monsieur... Feel free to vote for Napoleon as First consul or else......

The council members got out of Paris as fast as they could. They set up a new meeting place in the village of St Cloud, just outside Paris. But by the time Napoleon went to see them again the next day, the council members had found out that the story of the rebellion was a great big trick. They were furious.

This, according to the official record of the council, is what happened when Napoleon came into the council chamber:

DEPUTIES (rushing forward trying to grab Napoleon): *Tyrant! Dictator!*

OTHER DEPUTIES (waving pistols and knives): *Kill him!*

SOLDIERS (outside): *Listen to that noise! The general's in danger! Quick! We've got to save him!*

Soldiers rush into the chamber. Surround Napoleon to keep deputies away.

Deputies seeing soldiers panic. One soldier gets stabbed in the arm protecting Napoleon.

DEPUTIES: *They've come to kill us all!*

Several deputies jump out of the window.

DEPUTY: *I'm getting out of here!*

A few deputies stayed. Those that stayed voted to form a new kind of government with Napoleon in charge.

It was to be a government of three Consuls – an idea Napoleon got from reading about the ancient Roman Republic – with himself as First Consul.

Napoleon organised an election – a referendum – to see whether the people of France approved. 1,500 people voted against the new government, but three million voted in favour. It looked as though Napoleon was the people's choice, but in reality he was now the military dictator of France.

Chapter 5

Brilliant Soldier – Brilliant Organiser

Napoleon's first job as Consul was to defend France against the armies of the coalition – Austria, Britain, Sicily, Turkey and Russia. He needed a big victory which would make his enemies want a truce rather than continue with the war. Napoleon decided that the weakest part of the alliance was the Austrian army in northern Italy. However, the Austrian army was expecting an attack.

What Napoleon did was the one thing the Austrian's weren't expecting. Instead of attacking over the border, he marched his army into Switzerland and over the Alps and attacked the Austrian army from behind, near a village called Morengo.

The French army won. Later in the year, they beat another Austrian army at the Battle of Hohelinder in Germany.

Just as Napoleon hoped, the Austrians asked for peace and the coalition fell apart. In order to get peace, Austria gave France not only northern Italy, but also Belgium and some German states.

The next year, 1802, Napoleon held another election. This time he asked the French people if he should become Consul for Life. Eight thousand said: "No". However three-and-a-half million said: "Yes". Napoleon was now – in all but name – king.

Now that France was safe from attack, Napoleon began sorting out the messes that had been left behind by the Terror, the rule of the Directors and all the wars.

He found the cleverest accountants, lawyers and thinkers in France to help him and set to work. In five years he completely changed the way France was run in almost every way:

The law was a complete mess. Every little area of France seemed to have its own laws and customs. Napoleon, with his advisors, started from scratch and devised a whole new system of laws, called the Napoleonic Code. It's still the basis of French law today.

He completely changed the education system, opening hundreds of new secondary schools called lycées which were run like the military school he'd gone to at Brienne.

He introduced a national curriculum that all French schools had to follow, and a school-leaving certificate called the *Baccalauréate*, which is still the French leaving certificate today.

 He reformed the tax laws, and the system of tax collecting. For the first time in years, taxes actually came to the government instead of disappearing into the pockets of the tax collectors.

 He even made peace with Britain (although it only lasted a year).

Napoleon's Clothes

If you'd been living in Paris in, say, 1802 and seen Napoleon you would never have guessed from his clothes that he was dictator of all France.

Most kings, emperors and dictators like to show how important they are by wearing fancy uniforms, covered in medals and decorations. Napoleon was quite the opposite. He didn't like display, or spending money on clothes or fancy living of any sort. He liked plain clothes, and would keep the same clothes for a long time.

He had a particular "uniform" that he always wore:

 A flannel vest and short cotton pants – maybe four or five years old (remember, Napoleon didn't believe in spending money on clothes).

 A plain linen shirt and white silk stockings.

White cashmere breeches, held up by braces.

If in Paris, shoes with small gilt buckles. Napoleon didn't like new shoes, because he had very delicate feet. Whenever he bought a pair of new shoes, he made a servant with the same size feet wear them for two or three days to "break them in" for him.

If he was at home, his favourite footwear were slippers made of soft green or red morrocan leather which he would wear until they fell to pieces.

If he was on campaign, Napoleon wore plain black leather riding boots.

A long white cashmere waist-coat.

A muslin cravat.

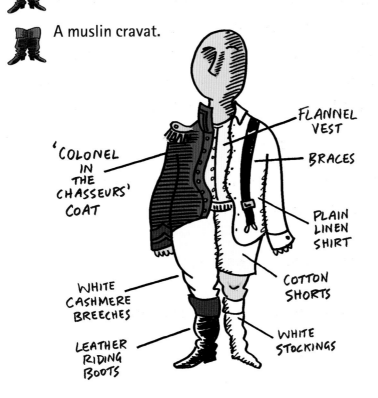

'COLONEL IN THE CHASSEURS' COAT

FLANNEL VEST

BRACES

PLAIN LINEN SHIRT

WHITE CASHMERE BREECHES

COTTON SHORTS

WHITE STOCKINGS

LEATHER RIDING BOOTS

The plain frock coat of a Colonel in the Chasseurs. It had gilt buttons and a scarlet collar, but no lace or embroidery. He usually kept his coats and breeches for up to three years.

A bicorn (two-cornered) hat made of beaver fur. He always wore his hat outdoors, and carried it in his left hand when he was indoors. His hat had another purpose apart from keeping Napoleon's head warm: when he lost his temper, he would often throw his hat on the ground and jump up and down on it.

But what was Napoleon really like? He lived at a time before there were celebrity magazines such as *Hello* and *OK*, or tabloid gossip columns. (These persuade members of a famous person's family or people who work for them to give interviews on the celebrity's private life.)

But this is what some of the people who knew Napoleon best might have told a journalist from:

Bonjour!

Le Premier Journal des Étoiles

His valet, Constant

Exclusive to
Bonjour!
Days in the Life of those closest to our heroic General Napoleon

His secretary, Méneval

His chef

THE START OF A TYPICAL DAY

By Napoleon's Valet

My name is Constant, and I'm valet to the First Consul, General Napoleon Bonaparte. That means I'm his personal servant, and I look after the General in all matters – and I do mean in all matters. I run his bath, help him dress, and make sure that he has all the little things that a gentleman needs to get him through the day – like his snuff box and perfumed handkerchiefs.

I normally get up just before 5.30 am. After I've dressed, and before I wake the General, I always check that the other servants have lit the log fires in all eight rooms of General and Madame Bonaparte's apartment. As you may know, the General was born on the island of Corsica in the Mediterranean, and he's ever so sensitive to the cold. He likes blazing log fires all year round – summer and winter.

> **"My brains work best at dawn, Constant."**

Then I go and wake him between six and seven o'clock. The General likes to get up early. He often says to me: "My brains work best at dawn, Constant."

The General and Madame have separate rooms –

of course – but they always sleep in Madame's room. So I take in his dressing gown – white cotton in

summer and swans' down in winter – and his leather slippers. He loves those slippers! He'll wear a pair until they're falling off his feet in strips.

Then we go up the small staircase to the General's room, where I'll serve him a cup of tea if he wants a hot drink, or a glass of orange-flower flavoured water if he wants something cooling. Then, while I'm running his bath, he'll open his letters and look at the newspapers – but it'll only be

a quick glance, because reading the newspapers is my job.

The General loves hot baths – and long ones, too. Usually he'll lie in the bath for an hour – topping it up with hot water – while I sit by the tub reading the newspapers to him. He sometimes has the bath so hot that I can't see to read the newspapers for the thick clouds of steam.

After his bath the General shaves. Now here's an unusual thing – I've known many fine gentlemen in my time, but the General is the only one I've ever come across who always shaves himself! Now you must promise not to tell anyone else what I'm going to tell you: although we're at war with the awful English, the General will only shave with English razors – enemy razors! Always the same ones, with pearl handles made in a place called Birmingham. You mustn't repeat this, but the General says that French steel isn't good enough! Then he'll ask me if I think he's shaved himself close enough. But he always has. I tell you, if things go badly for him in the future, the General could always make a living as a barber!

You'd think the General would be clean enough by now, after having an hour-long bath, wouldn't you? But oh, no. The General's very particular about keeping clean. Now he'll wash his face and neck with soap and wash his hands with almond paste, before cleaning his teeth.

"He's got beautiful white teeth"

He's got beautiful white teeth, has the General. He's got his own dentist, M. Dubois, but he's never needed him. The General always cleans his teeth twice – once with toothpaste, then with powdered coral. Then he'll scrape his tongue with a silver scraper – like the gentleman he is – and finish off with a mouthwash of water and brandy.

Has the General finished his washing? No! Next, he strips to the waist and I have to pour eau-de-Cologne all over his chest and back and scrub him with a stiff bristled brush. Only then is he ready to get dressed. By that time, I feel like I've done a full day's work and it's not even 9 o'clock…

A WORKING DAY

By Napoleon's Secretary

…and that's when my working day begins. My name is Méneval, and I am the General's secretary. Constant thinks he works hard, but I say no one works harder than me – except the General, of course. He is an extraordinary man – the work he gets through in a day – and I, being his secretary have to write down every decision, every note, every letter.

"My brain works so fast"

You see, the General dictates everything to me. He's often said to me: "I could never write everything down myself, Méneval. My brain works so fast, my hand could never keep up." My hand can barely keep up – even though I'm taking everything down in shorthand.

But there's another reason that the General doesn't write – and you must promise not to tell anyone. The General's

"The General's writing is appalling."

handwriting is appalling. When he tries to write fast it looks like a spider's fallen in the ink and then run all over the page. And his spelling – that's even worse than his handwriting! I suppose it's because the General was born on Corsica, and the first language he learnt was Italian. But even that's no excuse for some of the mistakes he makes. The other day he even spelt Madame Bonaparte's family name wrong – as he always does.

We work in his study. It's a lovely room, with huge windows looking over the palace gardens and the River Seine – or so I'm told. I never get to see the view myself. I sit at a desk in front of the window, but with my back to it. And with the speed the General works I'm lucky if I have time to breathe, let alone snatch a glance out of the window.

Many people walk up and down when they dictate. The General marches. Up and down the room, up and down, like a soldier on parade. For eight or ten hours a day! He must walk miles and miles.

But it's an extraordinary experience, listening to him dictate. He never seems to lose the thread of what he's thinking and saying. Other people would lose concentration once in a while and say: "What did I just say, Méneval?" or "Where was I, Méneval?" But the General – never! And he dictates a letter or a note just like he talks. So it's like listening to a conversation. Sometimes I have to look up from my work to make sure that General Murat – or whoever he's writing to – isn't there in the room with us.

He'll take a quick lunch at eleven o'clock, but there's hardly time to write up a fraction of what he's dictated, before we start again. It's a blessing when he has a Council meeting to go to, and then I can catch up on some of the backlog.

And when they day's finished, and I fall into bed exhausted, am I allowed to rest? No! Sometimes he'll wake up in the night and remember something he needs to write urgently. Will he write it out himself? Will he wait until the morning? No. He'll wake me up and off we go again, him striding up and

"Why do you work so hard?"

down the study and me taking down dictation at top speed. After a couple of hours, when his throat's dry and my wrist's aching, he'll order a couple of water-ices from the kitchen to refresh us. Then, as soon as we've finished the ices, he's off again.

Once I asked him: "Why do you work so hard?". He just pointed to himself and said: "The ox has been harnessed, and now it must plough."

NAPOLEON'S CHEF

They complain – but they are merely servants. Whereas I am a great artist! I am the best chef in the whole of France – which means, of course, I am the best chef in the whole world. So naturally, I am the General's personal chef… and all my skills are wasted!

You see, the General hates luxury. A General who hates luxury and the fine things in life – have you heard of such a thing?

He dresses like an ordinary soldier and eats like a peasant – but please don't tell anyone I said so. Do you know what his favourite food is? Go on, guess… Beans and potatoes! And what does he drink with his food – cheap plonk bought from the local grocer!

"I am a great artist!"

Now I know we shouldn't talk about the old days – when you-know-who was king – but I used to cook for royalty. Yes, the Duke of Bourbon himself! Now there was a man who appreciated good food, good wine – and a good chef. But the General…

The other week I cooked a dinner – only four courses: soup, grilled fish, chicken fried provençale style, and dessert – that the old Duke would have thought just a light snack between meals.

The General called me in when dinner was finished. (He gobbled it up in less than half an hour, as usual).

I was expecting him to say: "Well done. Delicious!" But what did the general say? "You've made me eat too much." A wonderful meal and he's annoyed! "From now on, no more than two courses – understand?" I was about to leave, but he called me **"And no more garlic!"** back. "And no more garlic in the fried chicken. I don't like the taste of garlic."

I didn't know what to say. The ruler of France and he doesn't like the taste of garlic! I said to him, "So what would you like me to cook?"

He looks me straight in the eye – me, the best chef in the whole of France, remember – and says: "Pork sausages."

But the General likes men who speak their mind. So I said to him, straight out: "But that's peasant food, General. If I serve you sausages you'll be up all night with indigestion."

"Sausages," he repeated. "I want you to cook me sausages."

So I did what he asked – well, almost. I couldn't bring myself to cook that revolting pork rubbish, so – quite brilliantly, I thought – I made him the most delicate and delicious sausages from minced partridges. Exquisite! They took me all day to prepare. And what happened when they were served? He flew into a rage and kicked the table over!

That was it! Enough!

"I resign!" I said.

"Good!" said the General. "No more garlic!"

The next day, the General's master of the household came to see me. "You're both great men," he said to me. "You deserve to be the General's chef, and he deserves the cooking of the

greatest chef in all of France – you. A little give and take is all it needs, a little give and take…"

Finally he persuaded me to stay. So that night, as a peace offering, I cooked one of the General's favourite dishes: plain roast chicken, no garlic. Bah! But as the master of the household had said: "A little give and take…"

At the end of the meal, the General called for me again. And he reached out and gave

"The greatest chef in all of France"

me a pat on the cheek, and grinned at me just as if we were the oldest of friends.

...if there had been such a magazine...

But even at times of peace, Napoleon always had enemies who were plotting, trying to make trouble – in particular Britain. The British government was always trying to persuade other countries to join them in a war against France. And it was always ready to give money and encouragement to royalist groups inside and outside France who wanted to make trouble. It was always ready to help anyone who had a plot to...

Chapter 6

Kill Napoleon

Sometimes something really small – like one glass of wine too many, or a fancy scarf – can change the course of history.

It was Christmas Eve. There was to be the first performance of Hayden's great oratorio *The Creation* that night at the Paris Opera House. Josephine, Napoleon's wife, and Hortense, his step-daughter, wanted to go. Napoleon, who'd had a hard day (as usual) didn't. He wanted to rest in front of a log fire at home, not go out in the cold. Eventually, Josephine managed to persuade him to come with them: "It'll do you good," she said.

As usual, the family were to travel in two coaches: Napoleon in the front coach; Josephine, Hortense and some friends in the second. As they were about to get into the coaches, Josephine stopped to rearrange her scarf. Napoleon, impatient as always, told his coachman to drive on.

They drove across the square in front of the palace towards the narrow street that led to the Opera.

Partly blocking the street was a horse and cart. On the cart was a large beer barrel. In the darkness, no-one noticed a man on the cart strike a flint, then jump from the cart and run away as fast as he could.

As it was Christmas Eve, César, Napoleon's coachman, had been celebrating with some of the other servants. Maybe he thought he was going to have the night off. He was usually a careful driver, but a couple of glasses of wine made him bold.

Instead of slowing down or stopping at the obstruction, César drove the horses through the narrow gap between the cart and the wall at top speed and into the street beyond. That may have saved Napoleon's life, because as the coach sped down the street the gunpowder packed into the barrel on the cart behind them exploded.

If the second carriage had been right behind, it would have been blown to smithereens. But because Josephine had been delayed, fiddling with her scarf, her carriage was still some distance away from the cart when it blew up, so she and Hortense and the rest of their party escaped with just a few cuts and bruises. But the people in the houses nearby weren't so lucky. The huge explosion ripped through the houses and nine people were killed.

Napoleon may have been the dictator of France, but the assassination plots showed him how vulnerable he was. Most kings and emperors weren't as powerful as he was, but when a king or emperor died there was never a gap. The very second they died a new king or emperor was created in their place. It was the ancient cry:

"the king is dead – long live the king!" But when Napoleon died, there would be no-one to take his place.

Napoleon decided that the only thing he could do to protect France and the Empire was to make himself an emperor, just like the Emperor of Austria or the Tsar of Russia. That meant that when he died, his title of Emperor would be passed on to his heir – a son, if he had one, a brother if he didn't. Even if Napoleon was dead, France would still have a ruler: the next emperor.

Emperor

Beethoven, the great German composer, was a big fan of Napoleon. Even though Napoleon was French and Beethoven was German, Beethoven had wanted Napoleon to win the wars against Austria and Prussia. This was because Napoleon had promised to get rid of feudalism and all the old, unfair laws in a lot of Germany. Like Napoleon, Beethoven was a passionate believer in the ideals of the French Revolution.

Beethoven had just finished writing a new symphony. It was the largest, grandest, most revolutionary symphony ever written. He was going to call it *The Napoleon Symphony*, in honour of his hero. It was all ready, the dedication had even been written on the title page of the manuscript.

There was a knock at the door. A friend had arrived at Beethoven's house to tell him the astonishing news: "Napoleon has crowned himself Emperor."

At first, Beethoven refused to believe it. Then he flew into a dreadful rage, seized his pen, and with vicious gouges of the nib – as if he wanted to stab the Emperor himself – Beethoven scored out both the dedication and the title.

All over Europe, supporters reacted to the news in the same way as Beethoven – with disbelief, disgust and anger. It wasn't just disappointment; they felt betrayed.

Invade England!

But if Napoleon had been expecting a new respect from his fellow monarchs now that he was an emperor, he was mistaken. They were livid! They didn't see him as an emperor at all, they thought he was an imitation – "upstart" they called him.

And Britain was causing trouble again. The British government was once again at war with France and looking for allies. In 1805, Britain formed a new coalition with Russia and Prussia. Napoleon knew there could be no peace while Britain and her navy were free. Napoleon decided that the only solution was to invade England.

Secretly, Napoleon began to build ships and get an army together. By the early autumn of 1805, there were 100,000 French troops and 2,000 ships near the channel port of Bolougne ready to invade. But, first, the British navy, which was protecting the English coast, had to be got out of the way.

Napoleon's plan was simple: cause a diversion; lure the English ships away from the coast and into the open sea and leave the way clear for the invasion.

Putting together the finest ships from both the French and Spanish navies Napoleon ordered his ships to sail – not across the channel but in the opposite direction. The plan seemed to be working, the English navy followed. They chased the French and Spanish ships round the coast of France, south into the Atlantic Ocean.

Battle of Trafalgar

And that's where Napoleon's plan went horribly wrong. The English caught up with the French and Spanish fleet, near a cape on the coast of southern Spain called Trafalgar. Although the English commander, Admiral Nelson, was killed during the battle, the French and Spanish fleet was totally destroyed.

Napoleon had not only failed to destroy the English navy, but now he hadn't enough ships left to take his soldiers across the channel. The invasion of England had to be called off... again.

A European Empire

But things were very different for Napoleon on land. Literally turning his back on England, Napoleon marched his army from Boulogne into the middle of Europe to fight his other enemies: Russia, Prussia and Austria. On land he had his three greatest victories yet, the first of them just two months after the defeat at Trafalgar.

EUROPEAN CUP 1805–1807
FRANCE vs REST OF EUROPE

... FIRST ROUND: Austerlitz, December 2, 1805... 68,000 French troops, under the command of the Emperor, defeats 90,000 troops from both Russia and Austria... Enemy trapped on Pratzen Plane, 15,000 killed & 11,000 captured...

SECOND ROUND: Jena, October 14, 1806... 122,000 French troops, commanded by Napoleon, destroy the Prussian army...

THIRD ROUND: Friedland, June 14, 1807... Crushing defeat for Russians from French army, commanded by Napoleon.

Once again, Napoleon's victories had brought peace and new territories for the Empire. But Napoleon knew that the war wasn't over, it was just another truce; the Final was still to be played.

The Secrets of Napoleon's Success

The "secrets" of Napoleon's military success didn't change much over the years. They were:

- break the rules of war
- fight to win
- keep your soldiers under control – if you can't control them before or after a battle (looting, stealing etc.) you won't be able to control them during a battle and the ordinary civilians – who you are probably saving from the enemy – will hate you
- try to make things better for the citizens after you've conquered their country than they were before. Give them the good things from the revolution, such as no more feudalism, and fair laws and taxes
- don't turn your back on them – leave somebody you trust in charge to run things after you leave – preferably a member of your immediate family or one of your best friends

Being Part of the Empire

Napoleon didn't rule the whole Empire himself from Paris. When he either conquered a new territory or was given it as part of a peace treaty, he got rid of the old rulers and set up a new state which had many of the good things of the French system. And when he got rid of the old rulers, he often replaced them with either members of his family or his closest friends.

Napoleon's dream was to rule an Empire where the laws were fair to everyone, there were no special privileges for nobles or clergy, the citizens of each country elected their own parliaments and everyone could follow the religion of their choice.

What stopped his dream from coming true were the constant wars. To pay for the wars, Napoleon had to raise very heavy taxes and force young men from all over the Empire into the army.

So despite all the good things the Empire gave them, the people of Westphalia, Italy, Holland and the rest hated the Empire because of the high taxes and their young men being forced to fight in the French army.

Napoleon decided to try and stop the wars once and for all. He knew that another huge war was inevitable, but this time he would try and utterly destroy one of his most powerful enemies before they had a chance to attack him first. He'd never lost a battle on land, so he was confident that he could win such an enormous victory that no-one would ever dare to threaten him again.

He decided to invade Russia.

War in a Wasteland

Napoleon gathered troops from all the Empire into what he called The Grand Army. In June 1812 he led 650,000 soldiers into Russia.

The Russian army's tactics were brilliant. The Russian army retreated. They refused to fight, and Napoleon and his army were led deeper and deeper into Russia without having once fought a battle. As the Russian troops retreated, they burnt all the towns and the crops as they went. Napoleon's army found only scorched earth.

Because Russia is so vast, and so far from France, it was impossible for the Grand Army to be supplied with food and other provisions from France. Napoleon had been relying on "foraging" – stealing – most of what the army needed. But the Russian troops left nothing behind: no food, no shelter.

The French army reached Moscow in September, exhausted and hungry. Napoleon had been planning for the army to spend the winter in Moscow, and continue the invasion in the spring.

Moscow was the first city or large town the French had come to which hadn't already been destroyed. But once again, most of the people had vanished. Only a few hard-looking men lurked in the shadows of the buildings.

The first night the Grand Army spent in Moscow fires suddenly broke out all over the city. Napoleon's men searched desperately for hoses and pumps to put out the fires. They'd all been removed. They tried to fight the fires with buckets, but it was no good. A strong wind spread the fires from house to house and from street to street.

As Napoleon and his officers watched helplessly, the city of Moscow burned around them.

Napoleon turned his army round and started to retreat back to France. But winter had started, and the snow was falling fast. Suddenly Russian troops were everywhere, attacking the long line of exhausted, freezing French troops. Thousands froze to death in the snow, or died of starvation.

Of the Grand Army of 650,000 men who had crossed the border in June, only 40,000 got back to France.

Chapter 7

The End of the Empire

This was the moment Napoleon's enemies had been waiting for. Napoleon had been defeated and lost most of his army. They attacked from all directions. The Russian army attacked France from the east, Prussia from the north, and the British army invaded Spain and attacked from the south.

In 1810, Napoleon had divorced the Empress Josephine, who hadn't given him an heir, and married Marie Louise, the daughter of the Emperor of Austria. He was sure his own father-in-law wouldn't attack him; he was wrong.

Paris was surrounded and surrendered. Napoleon was taken prisoner. Under the terms of the peace treaty, Napoleon was banished to the tiny island of Elba in the Mediterranean.

As he was about to board the ship to leave France for Elba, he was surrounded by his old comrades – the Old Guard who had fought under him all over Europe. He turned to them and made this speech:

"Soldiers of my Old Guard, I bid you good-bye. For twenty years I have found you uninterruptedly on the path of honour and glory. Lately no less than when things went well you have been models of courage and loyalty. With men like you our cause was not lost; but the war could not be ended: it would have been civil war, and that would only have brought France more misfortune. So I have sacrificed our interests to those of our homeland; I am leaving; you, my friends, are going to go on serving France. France's happiness was my one thought; and it will always be what I wish for most. Don't be sorry for me; if I have chosen to go on living, I have done so in order to go on serving your glory. I want to write about the great things we have done together! . . . Goodbye, my children! I should like to press you all to my heart; at least I shall kiss your flag! . . . "

What a speech; what a performance! Everyone was in tears, including some of the British, Austrian and Prussian troops who were waiting to take the captured emperor into exile.

Today if a famous leader went into exile, journalists from all around the world would be clamouring for an exclusive interview. Let's just imagine that an intrepid reporter braved the journey to the island of Elba and returned with this scoop . . .

NAPOLEON:
THE Celebrity Questionnnaire

Q What's your favourite place?

A Corsica – where I was born.

Q What was your favourite subject at school?

A Mathematics.

Q What was your least favourite?

A Spelling and handwriting – oh, and dancing, too. I was always a terrible speller and a dreadful dancer.

Q What's your favourite food?

A Plain food – vegetables, potatoes, beans. I once had a dish invented specially for me: Chicken Morengo, named after my victory in the war against the Austrians. It was made up from a few ingredients – a chicken, tomatoes, a couple of crayfish – which my cook managed to find after the battle. Rather like your "Ready, Steady, Cook".

Q What's your favourite word?

A Three words: Freedom, Equality, Brotherhood.

Q Meaning...?

A It's the slogan of the Revolution. It means freedom for everyone from poverty and injustice, and from unfair laws. It means everyone is equal under the law – not different laws for the rich and for the poor. It means all men are brothers – no-one is born to rule over or own anyone else.

Q Who was the love of your life?

A France.

Q No, I mean a person.

A The Empress Josephine ... and my son.

Q But you divorced Josephine in 1810 and married the daughter of the Austrian Emperor.

A But that was for France. Josephine could not give me an heir. Without an heir the Empire would collapse after I was dead.

Q It collapsed anyway, even though you had an heir.

A Yes, I know.

Q What qualities do you most dislike in other people?

A Extravagance – a love of luxuries and expensive toys and clothes – and dishonesty. I particularly hate the dishonesty of politicians such as Talleyrand and Metternich.

Q What quality do you most dislike in yourself?

A Impatience. Maybe if I had been more patient, and we'd wintered in Moscow, I would not have lost the Grand Army. But then if I had been patient and waited in Egypt, I would never have become Consul and Emperor.

Q What qualities do you think others most admire in you?

A Firstly, energy. I can work all day and all night, and just take the odd nap when I want. Some people have said I must have exceptionally large lungs to have so much energy! And my memory. I can remember the faces and names of my soldiers years after the battles they fought in; and I can remember maps after just a quick glance.

Q What do you most regret?

A That I could never bring peace to the Empire so that everybody could enjoy the benefits of freedom, good laws and prosperity.

Q Who do you blame for that?

A The English!

One Last Try

Louis XVI's brother came back to rule as king Louis XVIII. (Louis XVII, Louis XVI's son, had died in prison just a few years after his father's execution.)

The nobles who had been living abroad came back. The new government was determined to get rid of all traces of the revolution. All the old privileges were brought back. The ordinary people hated the return to the old ways. They'd got used to living without lords telling them what to do and robbing them.

Throughout France people were saying: "Things were better under Napoleon. I wish the emperor would come back." It didn't take long for word to reach the King of Elba.

Napoleon slipped away from Elba secretly and landed in Marseilles in March 1815, with just a handful of men. He'd promised himself that if a single shot was fired against him, he would turn round and go back rather than have to fight a fellow Frenchman. He didn't have to worry. Everywhere he went, people yelled: "Long live the emperor!" As he marched north to Paris, more and more ex-soldiers joined him. The king fled. By June, Napoleon had an army of 72,000 men. But the countries against him – Austria, Britain, Russia and Prussia – were putting together six armies totalling almost one million men.

The British army under the command of the Duke of Wellington had already invaded Belgium and was waiting for Napoleon, but the two Prussian armies hadn't marched so fast and hadn't linked up

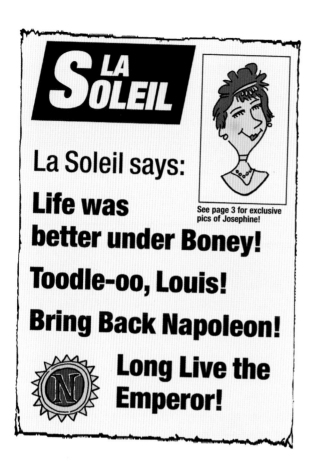

LA SOLEIL

La Soleil says:

Life was better under Boney!

See page 3 for exclusive pics of Josephine!

Toodle-oo, Louis!

Bring Back Napoleon!

Long Live the Emperor!

with the British. This was just the situation which Napoleon liked best – attacking his enemies before they were ready. On June 16th, Napoleon launched one of his surprise attacks on one of the Prussian armies, which was still several kilometres from the British army. He won. But on June 18th he attacked the British army near a small town in Belgium called Waterloo.

Napoleon's Waterloo

The battle began in the early morning. Although the weather was fine, rain had been falling heavily for several days and the ground was very muddy. Napoleon decided not to attack Wellington's main army until midday, to let the ground dry out a little. This was a fatal mistake. As Wellington admitted, if Napoleon had attacked early he would have won. By delaying, Napoleon gave the second Prussian army enough time to reach Waterloo. When Napoleon's troops

IT WAS THE NEAREST-RUN THING YOU EVER SAW IN YOUR LIFE.

finally attacked, they were now fighting two armies instead of one. Napoleon's army was outnumbered and defeated. But it could so easily have been another victory for Napoleon. The next day, Wellington called the Battle of Waterloo: "The nearest-run thing you ever saw in your life".

The prisoner of St Helena

Napoleon knew that if he was captured by the Prussians they would execute him. He rode away from the battlefield and returned to Paris. From Paris he went to the port of Rochefort, where there was a British ship anchored, the *Bellerephon*. He surrendered to the Captain, on the understanding that he would be taken to Britain.

But the British government didn't want him to come to Britain. Instead, the *Bellerephon* was ordered to take Napoleon to the tiny island of St Helena in the South Atlantic Ocean, 1,834 kilometres from the coast of Africa and 8,046 kilometres from France. Realising he had been double-crossed, Napoleon wrote a letter to the British government. This is part of it:

I hearby solemnly protest against this injustice... I came freely on board the "Bellerephon". I am not a prisoner. I am the guest of England... I gave myself up in good faith and claimed the protection of the English laws. If I am exiled to St Helena, it will impossible for the English to talk about their good name, their laws and their liberty. British good faith will have been lost... I appeal to history.

But Napoleon's appeal was ignored. Napoleon was kept prisoner on St Helena, guarded by a garrison of almost 2,000 British troops until 1821, when he died of stomach cancer at the age of 51.

Not the End

People die, but ideas have ways of living on.

In 1830 and 1848, revolutions started all over Europe. People in Italy, Germany and France hadn't forgotten what it had been like to have a country of their own under Napoleon's Empire. But this time, they promised themselves, it would be their own country, not ruled by a foreign lord or prince or Emperor. It was what Carlo Bonaparte and Pasquale Paoli had wanted for Corsica before Napoleon was born.

France didn't forget Napoleon's reforms, either. French laws are still based on the code Napoleon drew up.

And no-one in Europe could forget the French Revolution and its ideals: Freedom, Equality and Brotherhood. These ideas haunted the old emperors and kings, who desperately tried to go back to the old ways. But they couldn't work. The ordinary people remembered what it was like to be free of their lords and bishops. One day, they would elect rulers who would govern in the interests of the ordinary people.

One day there would be Freedom, Equality and Brotherhood for all!

Lifeline

1769 Napoleon is born in Corsica

1796 He marries Josephine de Beauharnais

1799 Napoleon seizes power in France

1804 He crowns himself Emperor of the French people

1805 He defeats his enemies at Austerlitz

1810 He marries Marie Louise of Austria

1812 Napoleon enters Moscow

1814 Napoleon is exiled on Elba

1815 He is defeated at the Battle of Waterloo

1821 Napoleon dies on the island of St Helena

Charles Darwin
and a selection of others (naturally)

Chapter 1

What did people think before Darwin?

Darwin? Who's Darwin?

It's a long story. First of all, here's a simple question. Where do you come from?

No, I don't mean, "I come from Ashton-under-Lyne," or even Stow-on-the-Wold. I mean – where do you as a human being come from?

No, I don't mean, "I was found under a gooseberry bush," or "the stork brought me," or even how it really happens (though we won't go into that now).

I mean, where do you as a *human being* come from, as opposed to where do you as a three-toed sloth come from, or where do you as a duck-billed platypus come from?

Well, I come from apes, don't I? They're the nearest to human beings. Some learned to stand up straight, use their hands, make tools, speak, put clothes on, and there you go – US.

Not bad. BUT – if I'd asked you that question at any time before 1859, what would you have said?

The same?

DEFINITELY NOT. If you were Christian, Muslim or Jewish, you would have said that you were descended from Adam and Eve. After God made the world in seven days, he made all the animals (birds, fish, reptiles and other creatures) and *then* he made human beings to be their masters. But Adam and Eve messed up in the garden of Eden, and we've regretted it ever since.

There's no time now to go into what you would believe if you weren't Christian, Muslim or Jewish.

Just a minute. Why did you say 1859?

Because that's when Charles Darwin published his great book, *The Origin of Species.*

Yes, but what about scientists before 1859? They didn't believe that, did they?

Yes. They saw things differently then.

How?

Nowadays – scientists believe their job is to find out what lies behind nature and use it if they can, both for our knowledge and our benefit. Or to blow us to bits.

Then – scientists believed their job was to find out what lay behind nature TO EXPLAIN THE WORKINGS OF GOD. Many scientists were themselves priests and clergymen.

There's a great difference. And here's what they believed.

a) The Earth, according to the Bible, was about 6,000 years old.
b) It had been made the way God designed it and had not changed. Nor would it.
c) All species were fixed. So three-toed sloths came into the world as three-toed sloths and three-toed sloths they would remain. The same applied to duck-billed platypuses. They had been like that for all time and that's how they would stay. This rule was so important that it was given a name –

THE IMMUTABILITY OF SPECIES.

Immutability?

Yes. Incapable of change. And why couldn't they change?

BECAUSE GOD CREATED THEM.

So there they were, all those prosperous people in the 19th century. They believed that nothing would ever change. They believed that they as human beings were special. God had created them separately from all other living beings. The world was like a great league table.

1. God.
2. Angels.
3. Mammals (including human beings).
4.
5. } *Absolutely everything else in the world to infinity.*
6.
7.

I reckon that if you could be sure of that, then you'd feel pretty good.

I suppose so. Did they?
Oh yes. As the 19th century got started, people really felt confident. Why, they knew nearly everything there was to be known. They'd explored most of the world. They'd found animal and bird species thay had never heard of and were on the look-out for more. They'd found savage tribes which needed civilizing. Who better to do it than your English 19th-century gentleman? After all, who was more civilized than him? A good reason to conquer half the world and call it your empire.

Besides, they had steam engines and great factories full of machinery. They could do pretty well anything they wanted to – so they thought. Why, one day they might even learn how to fly.

Oh, yes, they felt GREAT!

THEN ALONG COMES DARWIN AND SAYS, "IT'S NOT LIKE THAT AT ALL".

Well, what would you feel?

Gutted?
Probably. But would you believe it?

I wouldn't want to.
No, you wouldn't. Especially as it seemed to deny that God existed.

Well, doesn't it?
What do you think? It all depends on how you read the Book of Genesis about how the world was made. The Bible and Darwin can't *both* be right.

Or can they?

You tell me.
Later, later. Meanwhile, this is the battleground. Is it CREATION? Or is it EVOLUTION?

Evolution? What's that?

When things change and develop over a very, very long time.

So what's creation?

When things come into being separately, caused by a maker.

Evolution must mean that all life started from the same source – probably a tiny microbe in the mud when the Earth first began.

Creation certainly means that each being was made separately, with a purpose and as part of a great design.

EVOLUTION versus CREATION. Which was it to be?

★　　★　　★　　★

Chapter 2

Who made Charles Darwin?

His mum and dad, of course.
I know. But here's the first hint of what evolution may be.

Meet: On his father's side – ERASMUS DARWIN.

A very fat man. And brilliant as well. He was into everything: fascinated by the new canals, the first steam engines. He even wondered if all he'd been told about how God made the world and all the animals was really true. In 1796, 15 years before Charles was

born, he wrote a book – *Zoonomia*. In it, he worked out his ideas. Some people thought these ideas were mad, others that they were bad. Just a few thought they were wonderful.

But the time for these ideas had not yet come. Besides, they were only ideas. He had no proof and didn't know where to get it from.

Meet: On his mother's side – JOSIAH WEDGWOOD.

Ever heard of Wedgwood Pottery? Have you been to Stoke-on-Trent? Not just the home of Sir Stanley Matthews, the famous footballer, but of china cups, saucers and dinner plates as well. Josiah started it. In his Etruria Works he organized almost the first factory run on modern lines. Soon the 19th century would be full of industrialists like him. And the 20th, and the 21st – maybe.

So there we are. Two men years before their time, not afraid to change things and think for themselves.

Two generations later, Charles combined the qualities of both. That, very shortly, is what evolution is. Erasmus's son, Robert, married Josiah's daughter, Susannah.

Robert was a doctor and they settled in Shrewsbury. Robert was also a financial whizz-kid. Nowadays, he'd have gone to the City and made millions. Instead he stayed at home doctoring, investing his money and helping people into business. That was the time to do it. The Industrial Revolution was definitely on and there were fortunes to be made.

No wonder he had lots of patients. They might not get better but they could get rich. And Robert did too. Lucky for Charles.

Robert and Susannah had three daughters, Marianne, Caroline and Susan. Then came a son, Erasmus, named after his grandad. At last, in 1809, when Susannah was 44, Charles was born.

Forty-four? That's old, isn't it?

She had another baby, Catherine, 15 months later. You wait till you see how old Charles's wife was when she had their last baby. It wasn't much fun being a married woman in the 19th century. It wasn't a load of laughs being single either. In fact, it was best to avoid being a woman at all.

Now I come to think of it, Charles Darwin changed all that, too, though he didn't mean to.

★ ★ ★ ★

Chapter 3

A lab in the shed

Was Charles a clever child?
Far from it. More of a pain in the neck. He was an attention seeker. He broke things. He was jealous of little Catherine. Once he got on everyone's nerves so much that they locked him in a room as a punishment. But he tried to smash the windows. Caroline, his big sister, was supposed to look after him, but he was a real handful.

Why Caroline?

Susannah was ill. When Charles was only eight, she died. In those days, children weren't supposed to show grief. He bottled it all up. It changed him.

How?

He started collecting things. Anything – stones, shells, you name it.

He wanted praise, especially from his father. He never got it, so he just collected more things. The family had a greenhouse. Charles spent hours among the plants. They kept pigeons and he spent hours with them as well. Nobody guessed this was how he would spend most of his later life. His father decided he needed company his own age. It was time for him to go away to boarding school.

To Eton or Harrow or somewhere a long way off, I suppose.

No. Shrewsbury.

But he lived there already.

Even so, they sent him off to board there with his elder brother Erasmus. His father seemed to think this was a good idea. Charles definitely did not.

Shrewbury school was then a very small, very old place. It had a fierce headmaster, Dr Butler. There was no English taught (why should it be – everybody spoke English!); no science; a little maths. Most of the time was spent learning Latin and Greek.

Why?

Because that, Dr Butler believed, was how you became a cultured gentleman able to rule the country and also the world.

Sounds weird.
Maybe it does, but that's what public schools believed for the next century-and-a-half. People thought Dr Butler was a really way-out teacher of the future.

What was Charles like at Greek and Latin?
He *HATED* them. He longed to be back home. His brother Erasmus had fitted up an old garden shed as a lab. Here, in the holidays, they did experiments together and went on long expeditions looking for strange plants and weird insects. Then they learnt what they were and how to name them.

Yes, this was where he got his education, not school.

Why, what did finding out insects' names teach him?
It taught him habits of care and precision. The more he found, the more he wanted to know.

He sounds like a bit of an anorak. He'll be collecting Eddie Stobart lorries next.
Even if lorries had been invented, I doubt that. He was learning to be a 19th-century scientist. Collecting, naming, finding out. That's what science was then. There were so many new species to find, to identify. It's just as well they did. Half of them have since disappeared.

So he was going to be a scientist, was he?

Not yet. Charles was a great disappointment to his father. Dr Darwin thought his second son was a bit thick. Still, there was one thing he could probably do.

BE A DOCTOR!

Erasmus was already at Edinburgh University training to be one. If Charles went up to join him, Erasmus would keep him out of trouble and help him with his studies.

So Charles went to Edinburgh.

Chapter 4

Tiny details, big questions

Edinburgh. Freedom. Great!

Well, you'd have thought so. But it wasn't quite.

Yes, he loved the city, with the planned order of the new town and the higgledy-piggledy of the old town – 'Aud Reekie'.

He loved the country round about – Arthur's Rock, the castle, the Pentland Hills and the deep sea beyond.

He loved the people, always questioning, taking nothing for granted. And the plays and operas at the Theatre Royal.

And oh, he loved the food: herrings, fried oysters, cod's head with oatmeal...

But he HATED the medicine. When he watched in the operating theatres, he thought the sight of blood was a fearful thing. And when he had to dissect dead bodies – he threw up.

Before long, he was sure.

HE'D NEVER BE A DOCTOR!

Does that mean going to Edinburgh was a waste of time?
Oh, no. Far from it.

He walked along the coastline and collected cuttlefish and sea slugs, sponges and polyps.

He met a traveller, Charles Waterton, who'd been all over the world and told Charles what it was like in tropical rainforests. He also told him what a terrible thing slavery was. Waterton had brought a freed black slave back with him, John Edmonstone. John was a wonderful taxidermist – he stuffed animals – and taught the art to Darwin.

Charles listened to professors saying outrageous things which went against everything he had been brought up to believe. The minds of the lower creatures were really just the same as humans', and so were most of their organs, so there was nothing special about us. One of these professors Charles got on very well with – Professor Grant.

"Study tiny detail but ask big questions," Grant told Charles. And he never forgot it.

For the first time, Charles heard of an aged Frenchman, called Lamarck. He said shocking things as well. He'd spent his life looking at insects, worms, shellfish – and had decided that living creatures weren't fixed forever. One sort of creature could develop into another. The Church hated Lamarck. God had made every creature, they said. Nothing would ever change.

But Professor Grant told Darwin, "Don't listen to them. Lamarck is right."

And Charles began to listen.

Did Darwin not believe in God, then?
Of course he did. Big sister Caroline kept writing to him telling him to. Besides, he had to do something with his life.

He knew he wasn't going to be a doctor. But there was something he really could be.

A CLERGYMAN!

Yes, a lovely life as a vicar, with a nice vicar's wife and a nice vicar's house in an English village where he could wander round collecting insects to his heart's content – that would be *great*!

But how should he set about it?

Study somewhere else, I suppose.

Dead right. And if you wanted to be a clergyman there were only two places to choose from.

OXFORD OR CAMBRIDGE.

This was because in those days you could only go to either university if you were in the Church of England.

So he left Edinburgh and went to –

CAMBRIDGE.

A sleepy, windy little town on the edge of the wide, flat fens where rich young men went to have a smashing time and poor young men went to work their socks off.

Just like Oxford. Over the years, some things stay the same.

But in one way it was not like Oxford. Cambridge was a place of SCIENCE. It was then and it is now. As I said, some things stay the same.

In 1828, Charles Darwin went to Christ's College, Cambridge. But before that, something important happened.

★　　★　　★　　★

Chapter 5

A professor, a brown owl,
a beetle and a girlfriend

Something important? What could that be?

It was all very well being a vicar in a nice house, but it wouldn't be much cop without a nice vicar's wife. And back at home, three months before he went to Cambridge, he met:

FANNY OWEN!

"Aha!" he said to himself.

She was small and slim, with dark eyes and raven-black hair. She was lively. She flirted a lot and rode horses superbly. Charles took one look and said – "This is the girl for me."

So he got married, then.
No. He had to persuade her father first. Squire Owen was not going to let any hopeless young man run off with his daughter. Fanny's suitor had to have PROSPECTS.

Was being a country parson good enough?

Well, Fanny seemed to think so.

In all the many letters she wrote to him, she called him her 'postillion' – a sort of coachman – while she called herself his 'housemaid'. Everything seemed great.

No wonder Charles thought it was all sorted. But perhaps it wasn't yet.

Which was Darwin when he was at Cambridge – a rich boy having a terrific time or a poor boy working himself to death?
Neither. He didn't think much of the gambling, wine- and beer-swilling sons of dukes and lords. Also, to be a clergyman meant he didn't have to work very hard. He just had to get an ordinary Bachelor of Arts degree, the lowest Cambridge offered. A doddle.

So what did he do with his time?
He made good friends. Together, they had a great time. They formed a dining club called 'The Gluttons'. It had one aim – to eat food that nobody had eaten before.

Pictured here are some of the menus:

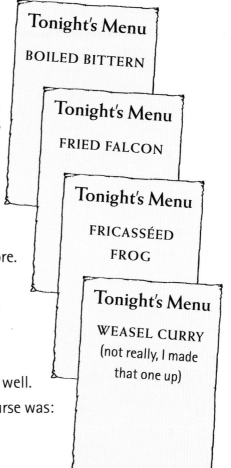

Tonight's Menu
BOILED BITTERN

Tonight's Menu
FRIED FALCON

Tonight's Menu
FRICASSÉED FROG

Tonight's Menu
WEASEL CURRY
(not really, I made that one up)

The Gluttons' Club was going well. Until, one evening , the main course was:

BROWN OWL.

They were so ill afterwards that the Gluttons' Club never met again.

But it didn't matter. A new interest was sweeping Cambridge:

ENTOMOLOGY!

Yes – butterflies, beetles, moths, more beetles – the Fens were full of them and Charles and his friends went chasing them. To good effect – they turned up several unknown species, killed them, brought them back to the college and set about identifying them.

Why?

Because science then was all about collecting and identifying species. The more people knew, the more they could wonder at God's wonderful creation. New species were identified all the time.

Nobody dared think they might have developed from old species. Oh no. Here, in solid Church of England Cambridge, the Bible meant exactly what it said and the world WAS created in seven days.

A great day came. Charles found a beetle people thought only lived in Germany. This was only the second time it had ever been found in Britain. Who could he tell?

Ach So..... mein holiday in Englande is over!

There was only one person. Professor Henslow, professor of botany but known to be brilliant at *everything*, very young compared with the rest of the Cambridge dons, who thought for himself and let nobody tell him what to do – even though he was a clergyman himself.

And thus began a friendship which lasted all their lives and had tremendous consequences.

What were they?
Wait and see. Meanwhile the three years passed pleasantly, and Cambridge came and went. Soon he would be a vicar.

He didn't worry about the science, what Professor Grant once told him in Edinburgh or what Lamarck said. He'd just read William Paley, a clergyman and scientist who wrote a brilliant book showing just how superbly God had designed the world and everything in it. What a great man, Charles thought. He couldn't possibly doubt now that everything had been created by God as part of a huge and wonderful plan.

How happy he was. He'd find a village to be vicar of, carry on with his collecting and see about marrying Fanny. But meanwhile, before he did anything else, he went on a big walking tour of North Wales, collecting as he went, looking at strange rock formations and wondering why God had made them like that. He only had one regret. He'd wanted to organize a ship to take all his beetle-hunting friends to Tenerife, that untouched, unspoilt tropical island, to explore the wildlife there. It didn't come off and Wales had to do instead.

But when he came home, he found a letter from Professor Henslow that would change his life.

More than that. It would change the whole world.

★   ★   ★   ★

Chapter 6

Sailing on the *Beagle*

Whatever could it be?

It was a invitation to go to sea.

So he'd get to Tenerife after all?

No. In fact he'd go almost everywhere *but* Tenerife. He was being asked to sail around the whole world.

Who by?

The Navy.

What had Charles Darwin got to do with the Navy?

Absolutely nothing.

I don't understand.

I'm not surprised. The captain's name was Fitzroy. The *Beagle* was a very tiny ship. Navy discipline then meant he couldn't be friendly with his juniors, so he had nobody to talk to. The last captain of the *Beagle* had killed himself through loneliness. Fitzroy didn't want to go the same way.

He asked his friend, Captain Beaufort at the Admiralty, to find someone he'd get on with to be his guest on the voyage. Beaufort asked Professor Henslow. Henslow thought of Darwin. Meanwhile,

Captain Beaufort went on inventing the Beaufort Scale, which is still used to measure the strength of gales.

The *Beagle* was a survey ship. Its job was to chart all harbours British ships were likely to go to and to find out as much as possible about far-off lands still unknown in Britain. Then we could trade with these countries, start church missions there – perhaps one day make them part of the British Empire. Fitzroy was a naturalist as well as captain. Darwin would be good company.

BUT – the voyage would last for years.

In the end, it took SIX.

What do you think Darwin said?

a) Did he say, "No way. I want to be a vicar. Besides, I've never been on a ship and I'd be seasick"?

b) Did he say, "No thanks. I want to marry Fanny and collect English beetles"?

c) Did he say, "Great. This is my big chance. I'll discover new species, make my name and be a great scientist"?

He's obviously going to say c), otherwise you wouldn't have started this chapter.

Dead right. But **a)** and **b)** went through his head and worried him a lot. Besides, he wasn't the ship's naturalist. The *Beagle* already had one, a man called McCormick, who was also the surgeon. When Charles set sail, officially he was nobody. Why give up everything just so he could spend six years cooped up on this tiny ship talking to a ship's captain he'd never heard of? They might *hate* each other.

But then he thought of exotic animals and birds never before heard of, teeming insects, great plains, huge mountains, steaming jungles, freezing wastes, vast continents and tiny islands and said to himself, "I've got to go".

On December 27th, 1831, *HMS Beagle* set sail from Plymouth, a little sailing ship on which there was hardly room to stand up.

So he didn't marry Fanny.
No. She'd been a bit distant lately. But when he left, he still had hopes.

And was he seasick?
Was he? He was terrible. He threw everything he'd ever eaten in his life back up over the ship's side. Perhaps the last bits of brown owl were among them.

Six years of this? Why did he start?

> *I joined the Beagle*
> *To see the sea.*
> *And what did I see?*
> *I saw the sea.*

Hold on, Charles. Things can only get better.

★　　★　　★　　★

Chapter 7

Right around the world –
part 1

Which way first?

Fitzroy's orders were to make a survey of the coast of South America.
So the *Beagle* headed west across the Atlantic.

SHIP'S LOG

300 miles west of Africa. Darwin has been
seasick all the way.

    Land sighted. Small island. St Jago.
We will stop there.

    Perhaps it will make him feel better.

Charles saw his first tropical plants on St Jago. He was amazed.

He saw something else too, which made him think. As he walked across the hot, dry plains, he saw a white band in the rock stretching for miles. It was made of corals and oyster shells, pressed hard together. But this was high above sea level. It must mean the sea had been there once. Why not now? Why had it gone? Had the Earth changed after all, or did God make it like that for some reason of his own?

St Jago was an old volcano. Did this mean that once upon a time this volcano had risen from the sea?

One man in the whole world thought so. He was back in London, his name was Lyell and he had written a book to say how the Earth's surface had gradually changed over millions of years. Not many believed him. They thought such ideas were shocking.

But Darwin looked at these shells high above the sea and said to himself, "*Lyell is right.*"

SHIP'S LOG

Atlantic crossed. Coast of Brazil in sight. Darwin has been seasick all the way. Still, he cheers up when he thinks about what he might find in South America.

Oh, the tropical forests and all the life in them fascinated Charles more than he could say. He started collecting specimens – plants, insects, animals. Especially insects. Weird creatures, like nothing ever even imagined before. They were preserved in alcohol, crated up and left in harbour for the next ship to take them back to England and Henslow. This was wonderful. But when they got to Rio, Charles had a *very nasty shock*. Letters from home were waiting. Charles opened his, only to read that –

I AM NOT GETTING UPSET!

FANNY WAS MARRIED!

That was quick.

Well, there you go. A rich man hoping to go into Parliament had been hanging round a lot before Charles left. As soon as Charles was out of the way he had proposed, they were engaged in January and married in March.

What a thing to hear on the other side of the world! Charles was grief-stricken. It didn't cheer him up a bit when he found out she had a rotten time as a wife because her husband was a bullying rat.

Come on now, Charles. Forget Fanny and just concentrate on the voyage.

"Don't worry," said Charles bravely. "I will." And he did.

The *Beagle* sailed on. And on. And on.

SHIP'S LOG

McCormick fed up. Wants to go home. Can't stand Darwin. So now we've got no naturalist and no surgeon either. Ah well, we'll just have to get on without him.

Is Darwin worth all this trouble? He is still seasick. Still, there is one thing. Now McCormick's gone, Darwin can be ship's naturalist.

Where to?

South. Always south. Down the South American coast. The tropics were left behind.

SHIP'S LOG

Off coast of Patagonia. Getting colder. Skies grey. Darwin seasick again.

Tierra del Fuego — 'Land of Fire' — close to. We have work to do there and cargo to deliver. We must chart the coastline and set up a Mission Station.

Tierra del Fuego.

When they landed – no more forests. Bare, barren land. The very end of the world. This was where the *Beagle's* last captain killed himself.

What was the cargo Fitzroy had to deliver? Years before, three people were taken from their hard lives on Tierra del

Fuego and brought to England. They had been given English names –
sort of. York Minster, Jemmy Button and Fuegia Basket. They had
learned to speak English and act like English people. Surprise,
surprise – they preferred this new comfortable life to their old one.
When Darwin saw where they came from, he was shocked. He wrote:
"How entire the difference between savage and civilized man is
greater than between a wild and a domesticated animal."

Nowadays, an explorer would look a bit closer and see there was
a culture as worthwhile as any others. But Darwin, like everyone
else, thought that no being on Earth was higher than an English
gentleman in the Church of England. That was why York, Jemmy and
Fuegia were going back, with an English missionary. They would start
a mission and turn the other Fuegians into Christian Englishmen,
because they'd see at once it was the best way to be.

In this they were sadly mistaken. Why? Darwin found something
to think about here which was very important.

What was it?
All in good time. Wait and see.

Now he wandered the Land of Fire. He looked at barren shingly
wastes and steep mountains, he found huge skulls and bones of
long-extinct animals – mastodons like huge elephants,
megatheriums like vast llamas, a gigantic armadillo – and all the

time he wondered – "How did they get here?" He remembered the
layer of shells all round St Jago. He'd just read Lyell's latest book on
geology. It said that landscapes altered slowly, some parts rising out
of the sea, others sinking below them.

Perhaps, millions of years ago, everything here had been very
different.

When they got to Argentina, Charles spent months riding across the great plains – the Pampas – still finding fossils and specimens, seeing strange birds and animals not seen anywhere else in the world, fascinated by everything he came across.

Then back to Tierra del Fuego.

How were Jemmy, York and Fuegia getting on?

Terribly. Or so Darwin thought. They only found Jemmy. He was married. York and Fuegia had gone away. All were living as they had before – and were liking it. The missionary was fed up and wanted to come home.

"Why?" Darwin wondered. They'd lived a lovely life in Britain, yet gone back to their old one. Why hadn't the Fuegians died out years ago in this cold, miserable land? Had they somehow adapted themselves to it over thousands and thousands of years? Perhaps they weren't so primitive after all.

Food for thought.

SHIP'S LOG

We have left Tierra del Fuego for ever. Round southern tip of South America, through Straits of Magellan and _NOT_ round Cape Horn. We're not stupid. Darwin more seasick than ever.

Turned north and sailed up coast of Chile. Days getting brighter and warmer. About time too. We'll dock first in Valparaiso. Plenty of British settlers there. Then we'll sail up the coast to Valdivia.

In Valdivia Darwin had three strange experiences. First – an orchard. Valdivia was surrounded by them. Trees grew very quickly here – all from little cuttings. Strange. Surely, he thought, if you cut a branch off a tree, it was part of that tree and would die with it. But these cuttings didn't. They became new trees. Nobody had noticed

that before. Perhaps all living things are like 'cuttings' from their parents.

Second – an earthquake. *The world, the very emblem of all that is solid, shuddered beneath our feet like a crust over fluid.* There was something to think about, because as a result – THE LAND HAD RISEN A FEW FEET.

Lyell was right. Some land rose while other land sank – and not just because of earthquakes.

Third – one of the greatest things to happen to him on the whole voyage. He crossed the Andes and saw one of the great mountain ranges for the first time. How did it get there? What incredible forces had made it?

But now it was time to leave South America. Charles said goodbye to it forever – but what he had found there would never leave him.

★   ★   ★   ★

Chapter 8

Right around the world –
part 2

How long have they been away now?
It's 1835. They left Plymouth over three years before. Would they ever get back? Yes. Before they left South America, Fitzroy told them they'd be home in 18 months.

Now Darwin had to think about what he'd do when he came back. But first –

Where?

A group of tiny islands in the Pacific, 600 miles off South America. They were 'frying hot', black, dead volcanoes sticking out of the sea. And on them – what strange wildlife! Turtles swam in the bays, giant tortoises lumbered round the land, 'disgusting clumsy lizards' slept on the baking rocks. Strange little birds like finches and bigger, uglier birds – sort of mocking birds. No insects. Odd.

Stranger still – the four small islands were very close to each other, but all the animals on them were different. Tortoises on one island had different shells from those on the others. The birds were all different. So were the few trees – each tree unique to its own island.

In the end, what he saw on the Galapagos Islands was more important than anything else on the voyage. But he had no idea of that then. Why they were different would come much later. Meanwhile, the *Beagle* had loaded up with tortoises and Charles happily ate them all the way to Tahiti, while the cook threw the shells with their different markings overboard.

Charming. And pretty ignorant, really. Civilization was certainly spreading fast.

Near Tahiti. Darwin so excited that he forgot to be seasick. Wouldn't mind living here myself. Captain Cook even passed through here a few times on his travels, before he came to a sticky end in the Pacific islands...

Charles loved Tahiti and was most pleased to see the Tahitian people so Christian and civilized. Why couldn't Jemmy Basket and his friends have been the same?

DARWIN WAS SICK HERE.... AGAIN + AGAIN + AGAIN.

Where next?

New Zealand (he didn't like it) then Australia. He wasn't sure about Australia. It would be 'a great princess in the South' one day, he said, but it was 'too great and ambitious for affection yet not great enough for respect'.

He never went there again. Just as well really if that's what he thought.

But they were well on their way home now.

SHIP'S LOG

Approaching the Cocos Islands. Here our orders are to find out all we can about the coral reefs there. Will they be good harbours for British ships?

As well as that — WHAT ARE THEY?

Charles was very interested in the coral reefs. He saw the smooth waters of the lagoons, the thousands of tiny coloured fish, the intricate branchings of the coral – and asked himself why.

Here is the reason he came up with. Some land rises, other land falls. These were volcanoes which were slowly falling under the sea. But the coral, a living thing, had risen from the volcano's surface and formed a round wall in the sea inside which the water could be smooth and green.

When Darwin came home, he'd try to meet the great Lyell and ask him what he thought of his theory.

Next came Mauritius, then Capetown (where he met the great scientist and astronomer Sir John Herschel. He was in South Africa for two years to map the stars in clearer skies than he got at Greenwich), back into the Atlantic and St Helena, where Napoleon had been exiled.

Nearly home now, then.

Not yet. Disaster.

SHIP'S LOG

Left St Helena this morning. Compasses should be pointing north. Instead they point west–south–west. We shall have to sail back to Brazil to check the longitude. Crew not happy about this. Tough.

Darwin seasick again.

Charles was cheesed right off. "I loathe, I abhor the sea." he said.

However, the extra voyage didn't take long and now England neared. But Charles had so much to think about. What would he do when he came back?

What do you think Darwin would do? Would he:

a) Be a clergyman as he intended when he left?

b) Find a woman instead of Fanny to marry?

c) Try his luck at being a scientist?

What would stop him doing a)? He was all for being a clergyman when he left.

Ah, but he wasn't now. He'd seen a lot which made him think hard. Perhaps there wasn't a great plan behind nature. Perhaps the Earth hadn't been created in seven days. It was changing and developing all the time. Perhaps species of animals and plants weren't made and fixed forever by God. Perhaps they could change and develop as well. Perhaps it was their surroundings which made them what they were.

Oh, there was so much to think about. One thing was sure. William Paley's book must be wrong. And if that was so, he couldn't be a clergyman. Not then, in the 19th century.

Surely he couldn't do b) yet. Had he got over Fanny?

Perhaps he never really got over Fanny. But whether clergyman or scientist, he'd need a wife. Besides, his elder brother Erasmus hadn't married. If Charles didn't, who would pass on the Darwin name? He'd better find someone, quick.

He'd do c), wouldn't he?

Not easy. Nobody knew him after so long away. He'd had no proper scientific training. Before he left, he'd only been collecting things.

Besides, what if his crates of specimens hadn't got back? What if his ideas about corals, rocks, plant and animal species were laughed at? No, being a scientist was not going to be easy.

But he'd soon have to make up his mind.

SHIP'S LOG

October 2nd, 1836. This morning we docked in Falmouth.

The voyage of the Beagle is over. Said goodbye to Darwin. Not a bad sort of chap after all. And there's one good thing – DARWIN WILL NEVER BE SEASICK AGAIN.

* * * *

Chapter 9

The new life and marriage

What did his family think of him now?

They saw a different person – six years older, a lifetime wiser.

They could see he wasn't going into the church. His father gave him £400 a year to live on. Not much? In 1836, very comfortable indeed.

Besides, there was good news. All the specimens had got back, they were full of things nobody in Europe had ever seen before and:

DARWIN WAS A SENSATION!

So was he a famous scientist now?
Wait a minute. Where was he going to live? Not Shrewsbury, for sure. The back of beyond.

Cambridge? Henslow was there, but nobody else. Too church-dominated.

No, it had to be London. He'd stay with Erasmus – for now.

Meanwhile, he must meet people.

First, the great Lyell – who thought Charles was great as well and said he must be right about coral reefs.

Then Lyell introduced him to all the other scientists of London, at the British Museum, the Zoological Society. Charles met them, listened to them and realized –

He was making enemies as well as friends. There were some who *hated* his theories. Especially when two fossils were found of monkeys millions of years old. "Aha," said Darwin. "Perhaps their tails dropped off in those millions of years and they developed into humans."

What a shocking thing to say. Being a scientist with new ideas was not going to be easy.

GOD DESIGNED EVERY LIVING THING AND THERE WAS AN END OF IT.

That's what you would think if, let's say, you were very, very rich. You owned huge country estates and a big house in London. You were probably a Duke or an Earl – a Sir at the very least. That God had meant it this way was something you would take for granted.

Would you want someone coming along and saying, "The way you think the world was made may not be right after all?" No, you would not. NOTHING must ever change.

Ah, but what if you weren't rich or titled? Let's see.

The Evolution Quiz

Let's see where you stand in the argument.
Tick the box against the answer that best describes you.
*Score: 3 for **a**, 2 for **b**, 1 for **c**, 0 for **d**.*

1. You are: ☐
   a. A duke. ☐
   b. A bishop, judge or some such. ☐
   c. A businessman on the make. ☐
   d. The poor twerp who does all the work.

2. You live in: ☐
   a. A castle.
   b. A mansion, bishop's palace or an exclusive house in the best part of town. ☐
   c. A big house near your factory. ☐
   d. A tiny two up, two down same as all the rest in the street, one loo and pump for water between you all. ☐

3. You have as much money as:
   a. Your vast estates bring in without you doing a thing to earn any of it. Remember, you and your friends own most of Britain and Ireland. But you have no idea how much it is. ☐

b. However much you get as the huge salary you earn in your high profession. ☐

c. You can, more and more each year you hope, from profits on your mill, factory, railway or whatever. ☐

c. Five shillings a week? You'll be lucky. ☐

4. When it comes to an election you vote for:

a. Whoever wants to keep things just as they are (e.g. The Duke of Wellington's Tories). ☐

b. Probably the same, though I'm open to argument. Or bribes. ☐

c. Anyone who'll let me get on and make whatever I want and do what I like without interfering (e.g. the Whigs). ☐

d. Vote? What's a vote? ☐

Well, how did you do?

If you scored 11–12, then it's long live the Church of England and may those scientists rot in hell. "God bless the squire and his relations and keep us in our proper stations," – that's the way to be.

9–10. If I thought that things might be a bit different, then perhaps I could get *right* to the top, along with those earls and such like.

8. Yes. The scientists are right. Just as things are not what we thought in nature all these years, they're not the same in Britain either. My father was nobody and I'm somebody, all by my own efforts. Nature's the same. If I can do better, so can animals. The game goes to the strong and the ruthless.

0. It doesn't matter what I think. Nobody hears.
(But they will, one day, they will).

Charles knew all this. The way his thoughts were beginning to take him made him VERY UNHAPPY INDEED.

So what did he do now?

For a start, he ought to get married. But who to?

Well, there were always his cousins, the Wedgwood girls. He really liked them. Especially the youngest, Emma. And lots of people married their cousins. What could be wrong with it? So, in November 1838 he plucked up courage and asked her.

He wasn't feeling well. He had a bad stomach which stayed with him for the rest of his life. But when Emma said "Yes," and seemed to wonder why he'd been so slow he felt much better. For a while.

BUT – Emma was very religious. Charles was wondering how he could ever believe in God again. Everything he saw took him away from what he was supposed to think. This kept him awake at night. How could he go on upsetting everyone he knew and loved? Was this what made his stomach so bad?

Anyway, on January 31st 1839, Charles married Emma and they settled in London, near the British Museum.

Was everything all right now?
Yes – but...

But what?
London seemed good for Charles. His work was there. All the scientific societies, museums and colleges were just down the road. How convenient.

Yet how awful. He never got a moment to himself. London was filthy. The streets were covered in horse dung. Emma didn't like it. Charles's stomach got worse. This was no place to have children.

What a year 1839 was. He got married, his book *The Voyage of the*

Beagle came out, his first child was born. A son called William. In 1841, a daughter, Anne. Charles should be so happy.

But he was always ill, the arguments in science went on and he knew in his heart that EVOLUTION was right, whatever the bishops said, whatever other scientists thought, however much it upset Emma.

There were riots in the London streets. People with nothing were beginning to get very angry about being poor when others were so rich. Would there be a revolution?

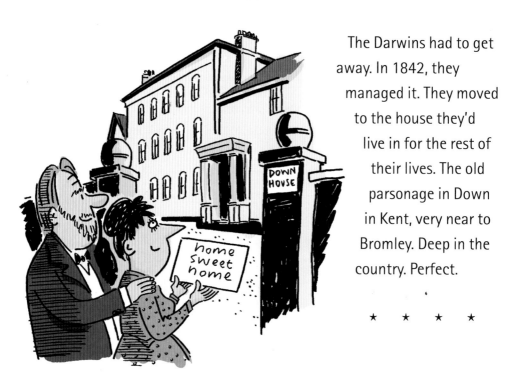

The Darwins had to get away. In 1842, they managed it. They moved to the house they'd live in for the rest of their lives. The old parsonage in Down in Kent, very near to Bromley. Deep in the country. Perfect.

★   ★   ★   ★

Chapter 10

Life at Down House

Was everything all right now?

No. Emma was having her fourth baby – a girl called Mary Eleanor. She only lived for a fortnight. Not a happy start.

Charles set up his study and worked hard. Books about rocks and insects, plants and animals poured out. All of them had the same idea behind them. Evolution.

But what made evolution work?

There was something more he had to find out. There were things he'd seen on the voyage of the *Beagle*, and especially in the Galapagos Islands that he couldn't quite get hold of. He wrote to his scientific friends, travelled to London for meetings, still couldn't quite understand. And he daren't write a book about all this. Not yet. The Church would hate it, nobody would speak to him, Emma would be very distressed.

Besides, someone had beaten him to it. In 1844, Robert Chambers from Edinburgh, not a scientist at all, wrote a book in which he outlined the whole evolution theory Darwin was working towards. He was horrified.

The book swept the country. Everyone was talking about it. Had he stolen all Darwin's glory?

No. Real scientists laughed at Chambers' book and Darwin knew why. It was only theory. Darwin knew his ideas were only theory as well. He had to prove them by long, hard experimentation. But on what?

Ah, he knew. Barnacles.

Do you mean those little shellfish which cling to the bottoms of boats?
Those are the ones. Down House was soon full of them, different

varieties from all over the world. Darwin dissected them, peered at them through his microsope and wrote notes. All his time was spent locked up with barnacles. His children never thought this was strange. "Where does your father keep *his* barnacles?" they asked their friends in the village.

At last, Darwin had his answer. Some barnacles were equally male and female, some were more male, others more female, some were completely male, others were completely female. He was looking at evolution actually happening. First, both sexes were in the same creature, then they gradually developed so in the end each was of a different sex. Barnacles made him certain he was right. Evolution was true.

Now did he wrote a book about it?
No. He still didn't dare. His stomach got worse. He wrote out his

ideas and locked them away with a letter to Emma to publish them only after he was dead.

Why? Did he think he was going to die?

Yes, he did. And in 1850 came something much more terrible. Charles was so ill that he went to Malvern for a water cure. The whole family went as well. But his daughter Anne, his favourite child, took ill there. Nothing could save her. She died. She was nine years old.

Darwin was grief-stricken. "Is my illness passed on from generation to generation?" he wondered. And then, "Why have two of my children died so young when they want for nothing?"

A good question. He'd come back to it later, especially as Emma was now 43 and having her seventh child, a boy called Horace. Now perhaps the time had come. All his friends said so. He started his big book on the great idea –

NATURAL SELECTION.

What's that, then?

It means that, through the generations, species change by tiny little degrees that you don't notice. The ones which keep going are those which change so that they can survive in the surroundings they live in. That's why wading birds have developed long legs, beaks and necks so they can stoop in the water, see fish, scoop them up and swallow them, while other birds have short, strong beaks to crack open shellfish or nuts. Creatures which adapt to where they live survive, those which can't, don't. Some animals thrive, others die out. Nature decides.

That was why tortoises and birds on one island in the Galapagos were different from those on others. They had stayed on their own island for millions of years, and adapted to those particular surroundings. Nothing ever came to upset them. Until man, that is.

Now Darwin wrote to farmers and animal breeders. They could make a new animal breed or a new strain of plant in a few generations with selective breeding. How did they do it? He started keeping pigeons and joined pigeon-fancying clubs, breeding pigeons with new combinations of colours and in different sizes. What he did in a few months, took nature millions of years. But nature did it in the end.

What about human beings?

Ah, yes. That was the big one. Had they developed from something else or were they really special and separate?

In 1857, an old enemy of Darwin's, Professor Owen, announced a discovery. He had studied the brains of apes and men. Human brains had an extra lobe in them, thus showing they were completely different from anything else.

Humans were different from any other creature. "I wonder," said Darwin, "what a chimpanzee would say to this?"

A WELL-KNOWN CHIMPANZEE REPLIES

Right. Listen up. You want to know what I think? Well. I'm disgusted with the lot of you. And I'm sad as well. I never thought I'd live to see such an ungrateful lot of grandchildren.
    You think you're so great, don't you? Well, answer me this.

Wouldn't you like to be able to climb trees and leap from branch to branch without a care in the world? Beats plodding round on the ground any day. You seem a right weak-kneed lot to me.

Wouldn't you like to be able to pick things up with your feet? Dead useful, that is, I'll tell you.

Wouldn't you like to be hairy ALL OVER, so you didn't have to waste time putting on those ridiculous clothes?

Wouldn't you like to be able to crack nuts with your bare hands?

And why isn't a nice pink bum good enough for you any more, answer me that?

Oh, it really grieves me to see you've thrown away nearly everything we tried to give you. I reckon it's been downhill all the way for you humans. I really worry about you sometimes. And let me give you a bit of advice. Don't let the gorillas hear what you think. They'd tear you limb from limb.

Yours more in sorrow than anger,

Charlie Chimp

"Well spoken, old friend," Darwin would have said if he'd read that. But he was too busy. All through the 1850s he experimented, observed and wrote. The GREAT BOOK was nearly finished. Then, in 1858, came –

THE GREAT BOMBSHELL.

★ ★ ★ ★

Chapter II

The Origin of Species

What was this bombshell?

A man called Alfred Russell Wallace. He was a poor man, but he'd read Chambers' book and Charles's story of the *Beagle's* voyage. He saved up enough money to sail first to the Amazon and later to Borneo, sending butterflies, beetles and birdskins back to collectors in London. He often wrote to Darwin and now he sent him a twenty-page letter in which he –

OUTLINED THE VERY SAME THEORY OF NATURAL SELECTION!

Poor Darwin. It looked as though someone was going to beat him to it. What could he do? Tear the letter up? Of course he couldn't.

Emma's eighth child, another Charles, was dying. Darwin was so full of grief that he couldn't think straight.

So he listened to his friends and did what they suggested. First, he outlined his own ideas and put them forward with Wallace's letter to a scientific meeting. So Wallace got some credit. But everybody now knew what Darwin really thought. He couldn't hide it any more.

He had to write a new book, shorter than the one he was doing, to put his ideas properly. He threw himself into work. He forgot his sadness over Anne and little Charles, he forgot the pain in his stomach and wrote and wrote and wrote. At last, in 1859, the great book was published:

The Origin of Species.

And the world has never been the same since.

Why not?

If Wallace was a bombshell to Darwin, to the rest of the world Darwin was like a giant asteroid the size of the Moon crashing into the Atlantic.

Think of it. Here's someone saying: "I know what you've taken for granted for the last few thousands of years is WRONG. You'll all have to think again."

It seemed to mean the Church was wrong, all religion was finished, everything on which people based their lives was swept away by ONE LITTLE BOOK.

Oh, dear. What would poor Charles do now?

Everybody read *The Origin of Species*. Bishops were scandalized, and half the world with them. The other half rejoiced. Some said that from now on, Science ruled alone. Others said that Darwin had done the work of the devil.

"We'll sort him out," said the bishops.

"We'll sort *them* out," said the scientists.

As for Darwin, he kept quiet.

But the scene was set. The battle lines were drawn. And now even the battlefield was chosen. The 1860 Conference of the British Association for the Advancement of Science, to be held in Oxford.

THIS WOULD BE THE GREAT SHOWDOWN.

But who would win?

In the red corner, for the Church and everybody who thought Darwin was the voice of the devil –

SAM WILBERFORCE
Bishop of Oxford and great at maths.

In the blue corner, for Science and the new way of thinking –

THOMAS HUXLEY AND
JOSEPH HOOKER

Scientists and Darwin's friends,
who were sure he was right.

Just a minute. Where's Darwin?

At home nursing his stomach which was feeling *especially* bad just now – and scared stiff anyway. Anyway, here's what happened at the meeting.

THE DARWIN SUPPORTERS' CLUB FANZINE

Special Report

Great Struggle at the British Association
A SPECTATOR'S VIEW

I'll never forget the events of June 30th, 1860, at the New Museum in Oxford. Some have said it was the biggest victory since Waterloo, and if you are a Darwinian, you'll definitely agree.

The great day dawned. Long before the meeting, the lecture room was overflowing and still more were pushing in. We all had to move to a bigger hall. The battle started. Darwin's friend Professor Henslow was in the chair. Two more friends, Thomas Huxley and Joseph Hooker, were on the platform. First, were some minor speakers. But we hadn't come to hear them. They were so boring we booed them off the stage.

Then came the crunch. The audience round me was hushed as one man rose to speak. 'Soapy' Sam Wilberforce, The Bishop of Oxford, great scholar, great mathematician, would speak for the Church. His supporters stood up and waved their handkerchiefs. They thought Darwin and his dreadful book would be put where they belonged.

But Huxley and Hooker needn't have worried. Soapy Sam soon showed that *he didn't know what he was talking about.* He didn't even begin to understand the book. I mean, the things he said. Crazy. Listen to them:

Why were animals mummified by ancient Egyptians the same as ours? Why couldn't scientists turn one kind of animal into another? Then he had the cheek to ask Huxley whether he was descended from an ape on his mother's or his father's side. Well, I mean. Ignorant or what? Perhaps he'd never even read the book. I think Huxley knew the battle was won.

Soapy Sam finished. Huxley stood up. First, he answered Soapy's points one by one. Then he said, in words I won't forget:

"A man has no reason to be ashamed of having an ape as a grandfather. If there were an ancestor I should feel shame in recalling, it would be a man, endowed with great ability and splendid position, who should use these gifts to..."

HOLD THAT ONE, SOAPY!

Then Hooker really put the boot in... Game, set and match to the Darwinians. Yet guess what? Soapy Sam seemed to think he'd won! What a twerp. Some of his mates thought it was a draw. Not from where I was sitting it wasn't.

YOUR SPECIAL CORRESPONDENT

Sounds great. I bet Darwin wished he was there.

Well, he did and he didn't. Back at Down House, he read the letters that Huxley and Hooker sent him about the meeting. Yes, he was pleased. But he was also afraid. He knew the real battle hadn't even started.

He also felt guilty. Yes, he was too ill to stand up for himself, no, he didn't like to think that others had to do his fighting for him. But he still worried about what people would say about him 'doing the devil's work'. Besides, Emma didn't like it.

★   ★   ★   ★

Chapter 12

And afterwards?

Was there anything afterwards? What more was left for Darwin to say?
There was plenty. *The Origin of Species* made everyone latch on to the idea that humans were descended from monkeys. But shall I tell you something?

Go on.
Darwin never mentions that in *The Origin of Species*, even though people called it 'The Gorilla Book'. In fact, he never mentions man at all. The book is all about plants and animals.

Is that so?
Definitely. Still, don't worry. Darwin was thinking about it. And
something else as well, which upset him very much.

What was that?
Marrying his cousin. No, he never regretted it. He loved Emma and
she loved him. It was just that –

What?
All his experiments with pigeons and talks with breeders and all his
observations showed him that the strongest stock came when the
parents were widely separated by birth. Breeders did not like in-
breeding among their animals. Cousins were very closely related in
the same family. Could it be that he and Emma were transmitting all
the weaknesses of their families into their children? Two had died,
one was retarded, none had the restless mind that he had – or
grandfather Erasmus had. Really, they were all a disappointment to
him. Could it be his own fault? And if so, why?

It's in the genes, isn't it?
Dead right. The bigger the gene pool, the stronger the person – or
animal, bird or whatever. We all know that and we don't have to be
scientists. But Charles Darwin didn't.

**That's a bit sad, isn't it? It means his theories don't matter
anymore.**

Dead wrong. The amazing thing is how modern genetic theory shows how accurate they were. Yet there was still a long way to go before they were accepted. The battle raged on, and on and on...

Meanwhile, back at Down House, Charles thought that, since everybody blamed him for something he hadn't really said, he'd better give a bit of thought to where humans came from.

So where did they come from?

They came from apes. They gradually learnt to stand upright, they gradually developed reason and insight, their brains gradually grew, tiny little advances until modern humans appeared. So there was no great 'divine spark'. Humans weren't fallen angels, they were incredibly modified monkeys.

From
THE CHARLES DARWIN SUPPORTERS' CLUB FANZINE

THE DESCENT OF MAN
by Guess Who?

Well, he's done it again, hasn't he? This'll shut those bishops up once and for all. All right, so what if we are descended from monkeys? I reckon we've done well to get where we have and it's *much* better than having been there to start with, as our religious friends seem to think. So come on, Soapy Sam and all your cronies. Put up or shut up and bow to the evidence. And let's hear no more from you.

From
THE JOURNAL OF THE SOAPY SAM APPRECIATION SOCIETY

THE DESCENT OF MAN
by an agent of the devil

Is there no end to this man's effrontery? Spitting in the face of God and denying the Bible is one thing, to say that humans are not unique and separate from the rest of the animal kingdom is something else and absolutely horrifying. Still, I suppose in these strange days we must put up with terrible things like this. Besides there are some in the Church today who are beginning to think he might be RIGHT. Including our own Sam Wilberforce himself.

So perhaps I'd better just shut up.

Meanwhile, a well-known chimpanzee writes:

Dear Humans,

Welcome aboard. I knew you'd see it my way.

Yours,

Charlie Chimp

Was there such a row this time over his new book?

MAKE SURE YOUR FAMILY OBSERVE THE NOTICE!

DO NOT FEED

No. It was all dying down. As more and more scientists came to agree with him, so did the rest of the world. Just as well. Because Darwin was very ill. That awful stomach which had tortured him for most of his life was winning in the end. In 1882, worn out, he died at Down House, surrounded by his family.

He was 73 and now regarded as one of the most important people of the whole of the 19th century.

★　★　★　★

Chapter 13

Where shall we bury Charles?

Why ask? Did it matter?
Yes, it did. Charles wanted to be buried at home in Down. So did Emma. His wishes should be obeyed, she said.

But others thought different. He was a great man now. He was Britain's foremost scientist, who had worked out a theory which the rest of the world had accepted.

There was only one place:

WESTMINSTER ABBEY.

Here all the great and the good of the land were finally deposited. Darwin, his friends said, should be among them.

And everyone agreed. Queen, Prime Minister, the archbishops. Yes, the rows with the Church of years before were quite forgotten.

So on 26th April, 1883, a solemn funeral procession took his body to the Abbey, and there you can still see his monument today.

A great man who changed the world. Pity he was so scared about doing it at all.

★　★　★　★

Chapter 14

And now?

Does anybody now not believe him?
Quite a few. Some still believe it's all a load of lies. The Earth really was made in seven days, about 6,000 years ago, and then everything was washed away in a great flood, except Noah and two of every kind of animal. They are called Creationists.

Do all religious people people believe that?
No. Remember how, right at the beginning we wondered whether, in a sort of way, Darwin and the Bible could both be right? Well, there are many who believe they are. They believe that the story in the Book of Genesis, which is part of Christianity, Judaism and Islam is a MYTH,

which accounts for many things in a wonderful story. Other religions have their own creation myths. They remain wonderful stories and in them all is a nugget of truth.

But there's been so much new science since Darwin. Hasn't he been proved wrong by now?
A lot is clearer. Genetics has shown us how things work that Darwin couldn't understand at all.

But the basic idea, of natural selection, with nature modifying itself incredibly slowly as species adapt to new places and surroundings, remains the same.

And if nature develops, then society can develop as well. People needn't live in their 'proper stations' and women aren't inferior to men just because it's always been that way.

Change, change, change, always developing, always adapting. As with nature, so with the world we make for ourselves. Yes, Darwin didn't only change the way we see how nature works.

He changed the way we live as well.

★   ★   ★   ★

William Shakespeare

and other Elizabethans
from around the Globe

Chapter I

He Makes Me Sick

Rewind 400 years. Stop. Now go a little further back even than that.

Stop.

It's 1592.

Queen Elizabeth the First is ruling England and Wales. James the Sixth rules Scotland.

The Spanish Armada has been seen off. England is best. At least, the English say so.

London is where it all happens. And in a bedroom overlooking the noisy streets along the River Thames, a man lies in bed.

His name is Robert Greene. He is dying. And that's not the only reason he's not happy.

He calls for pen, ink and paper. He must write down what he thinks while he still can. He's got to get this off his chest.

He chews his quill pen as he ponders:
What do I want to say. What, precisely, is my gripe?

All I ever wanted to do was write plays. I've done a few and they aren't bad. Well, I don't think so, anyway. I reckon my *Friar Bacon and Friar Bungay* was a real cracker.

All right, I know others are better. My mate Tom Kyd's for one. That *Spanish Tragedy* of his would scare you half to death. And what about Kit Marlowe? His *Dr Faustus* really makes audiences shiver. Yes, those plays are about as good as you can get. Tom and Kit know what they're doing.

But what have we got now? Ignorant little twerps come along thinking they can do it all, thinking it's EASY. There's one in particular. Who does he think he is? Where has he come from?

Robert has made himself so angry that he's bitten the pen too hard and his teeth meet through the quill.

He's turned up in London from some place in the country nobody's heard of. He's only an actor. He's not one of us *real* playwrights. We ignore him.

He's had no proper education. He can't recite Latin and Greek until his ears fall off, like proper playwrights do. So he's *thick*.

There's a lot of rumours about him. Some say he's on the run because he poached some rich bloke's deer. So he's a *thief.*

Some say he's got a wife and kids back home and he's run away from them. So he's a *rat.*

Some say he's been in hiding because he's a secret Catholic. That really is serious. We should turn him in to the authorities. He could be spying for the Spaniards. Or worse. *The Pope.*

BUT NOBODY REALLY KNOWS.

Robert Greene pauses again. He still hasn't written a word.

I don't really care either, he thinks. As long as he doesn't write any more of those rotten, boring plays. People like him get the theatre a bad name. I mean, look at them.

What about his comedies? There's that *Two Clowns* – sorry, *Gentlemen of Verona*. Funny? I've read shopping lists I've laughed at more.

Can he write tragedies? Not if *Titus Andronicus* is anything to go by. I mean, nobody likes a bit of blood on the stage more than me, but, well – these disgusting brothers cutting a young girl's tongue out on stage, then her father cutting his own hand off, then baking the brothers in a pie and serving it up to their mother? *And she eats it.* Over the top or what?

All right, histories. I've never been so bored as I was with *Henry VI*. But as soon as it was finished, I found that was only the first part. So I sat through the second and that was *worse*.

"I don't believe it," I said. Well, I had to, because HE DID A THIRD. If you don't know when to stop, you're no good at plays, that's what I say.

Oh. dear! In his anger Robert has chewed off the end of his quill pen. He spits bits of feather over the bedclothes, dips what's left of the pen in the inkpot and starts writing.

How shall he put this? If it's too obvious he might make trouble for himself, but he needs to warn Tom and Kit and the rest to watch out.

He'll be devious.
Ah, he's got it. He starts to write.

> *There is an upstart Crow, beautified with our feathers, that supposes he is the only Shake-scene in the country.*

Is that clear enough? Is it strong enough? He chews his pen again, then speaks aloud.

"That Shakespere. He makes me SICK!"

He's tired. Time for a sleep. He'll finish the rest later.

As he closes his eyes, he remembers one of the first plays he ever saw. He sighs. "Ah, *Gorboduc*. They don't write them like that any more."

Well, he's asked the question. *Who was Shakespeare?*
But then, you might ask, *Who was Robert Greene?*
I'll tell you later. All in good time.

Chapter 2

Is this how it was?

We don't know much more now about Shakespeare than Greene did then. There were no computer programs to follow every detail of a person's life. Shakespeare was only born an ordinary boy in a tiny English town, so who'd bother noticing anyway? What there is has to be put together and made into a pattern like a jigsaw.

So we can start with **definites** and **could be's.**

First definite

William Shakespeare was christened in Stratford-on-Avon on April 26ᵗʰ, 1564. Stratford was a sleepy town in the midlands, hardly bigger then than a village is now.

First could be

Was he really born on April 23ʳᵈ? It's a strange coincidence that it's also St George's Day. (Though not a bit surprising that it's World Book Day as well.)

Second definite

His father was John Shakespeare, who made gloves and was a town councillor. John married Mary Arden. They had nine children. William was the third, but he was their first son.

Second could be

There was a grammar school in Stratford where boys could learn Latin and Greek, because that's what they needed to get on in life then. Girls didn't need to get on in life, so they learnt nothing. William probably went there, but not for long. His parents took him away because he needed to earn money to help the family. Every year the Shakespeares went to Coventry to watch the Miracle Plays. William never forgot them.

Third could be

Years later, after Shakespeare was dead, the son of an actor-friend of his told a story that as a boy William once worked in a butcher's shop and *"When he killed a calf, he would do it in a high style and make a speech."*

They did things differently then. Is this true? Who knows. This actor was known to be a bit of a joker.

After that – *nothing*. Until:

Third definite

In November 1582, a special licence was issued for William Shakespeare to marry Anne Hathaway.

Fourth definite

Their daughter Susanna was christened in the parish church in May 1583. Work it out for yourself. According to her tombstone, Anne was eight years older than William. So when they married, he was eighteen and she was twenty-six.

Fourth could be

He stole Sir Thomas Lucy's deer and had to get out quick. Where best to go but London? What best for him to do but be an actor?

Fifth could be

After his next child was born, a boy called Hamnett, poor Will decided he'd had enough. So what best but to run away to London and be an actor?

Sixth could be

But perhaps he didn't just run away from the family. Perhaps he went because doing something he was good at was the best way of making money. He sent money back to Stratford and often stayed there. In the end he went back to live. He bought New Place, the best house in the town. Sadly, it was pulled down in 1759 just to annoy people, by a theatre-hating clergyman. William planted a mulberry tree in the garden and this clergyman cut that down as well.

Seventh could be

William went away to be "a scholemaster in the countrey".
Where? Why not Hoghton Hall in Lancashire, as tutor to children
of a rich man called Alexander de Hoghton?

They still believe it there, anyway.

Eighth could be

The Shakespeare family were secret Catholics. Round about this
time, things got even rougher than usual for Catholics and, for
fear of being found out, the Shakespeares went far away and hid.

- **Where did they hide?**

Perhaps it was in Lancashire, in Hoghton Hall, where they were all
secret Catholics.

- **Is it true?**

I haven't a clue.

Definitely the last definite (for now)

In 1592, Robert Greene wrote nasty things about Shakespeare, the
London actor and playwright.

This means that, some time after 1583 but
well before 1592, Shakespeare came to London.

Chapter 3

What happened next?

What did Shakespeare do when he got to London?

One of five things could have happened. They are set out below. You must decide for yourselves. I won't give you any clues.

Did he:

a) Find nowhere to live and no job either, so he slept in a cardboard box in a shop doorway?

b) Go to Highbury and ask for a trial with Arsenal?

c) Turn up in Paddington Green police station and end up on trial whether he asked to or not?

d) Realise he didn't like London after
   all so went back to Stratford-on-
   Avon and was never heard of again?
e) Join a theatre company?

Right. Have you decided?

Is it a)?
Unlikely. Cardboard hadn't been invented yet.

Is it b)?
Unlikely. There is no record of a William Shakespeare ever having
a trial with Arsenal – or Spurs, Chelsea or West Ham. Or even
Wimbledon. However, much, much later Shakespeare did play for
Walsall, but they were only in the third division then.
  THIS IS TRUE. You'll know how later.

Is it c)?
Impossible to say. Police records were very poor then. This was
because there were no police.

Is it d)?
Unlikely. If it was, I wouldn't be writing this book. Although some
people would say it is true because they won't believe
Shakespeare wrote the plays. In fact they think *anyone* but

Shakespeare wrote them. They think a man called Bacon did. He was no relation to Greene's *Friar Bacon*. He was nothing to do with *Hamlet*, either.

Is it e)?
NOT NECESSARILY.

Yes, we know he ended up in an acting company. But did he join when he got to London or was he in it before? He could have joined when he was still in Stratford. Actors used to tour all round

the country, doing their plays in inn-yards. Perhaps Shakespeare
went one night. Could this be how it happened?

ACT 1, SCENE 1,
THE COURTYARD OF AN INN

The galleries and the yard itself are crowded. A colourful figure
appears. He is a herald and blows a fanfare on a trumpet.

HERALD

Tonight we give you the stirring play by our esteemed
friend Master Robert Greene, The Honourable
History of Friar Bacon and Friar Bungay!

ENTER THE PROLOGUE

The audience is hushed and rapt. A member of the audience
whispers to the person next to him.

SHAKESPEARE *(for it is he)*

This magic scene has opened up to show
A mirror of the world to any who
Will let their hearts and minds and eyes roam free
And soak themselves in all the riches here.

PERSON NEXT TO HIM

Are you all right, mate? You want to watch it.

ACT 1, SCENE 2

THE SAME

Friar Bacon and Friar Bungay is over.

*Audience cheers, claps and puts money in box on way out. Shakespeare has
remained. He sees the leading actor and goes to him.*

SHAKESPEARE

Excuse me sir, may I join your company?

LEADING ACTOR

Why, my likely feller-me-lad, we could do with a fine,
sprightly young jackanapes like yourself. Yes, my grand
young sprig of a shaver, climb aboard.

You can polish the Emperor Tamberlaine's spear for a start and make sure all the severed heads have fresh blood on them every night. Does that suit you?

SHAKESPEARE
It's all I ever wanted, sir.

LEADING ACTOR
Then ho! for London, fame and fortune for us all.

EXEUNT OMNES
(That's "everyone goes off" to you)

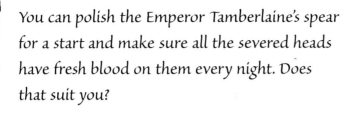

Well, it might have been. On the other hand, let's have a different second scene.

tamberlaine

ye metal polish

ACT 1, SCENE 2

Friar Bacon and Friar Bungay ends. Audience shouts, cheers and
claps wildly. Puts even more money in box on way out.

SHAKESPEARE
I don't believe it.

PERSON NEXT TO HIM.
I know. Wasn't it brilliant?

SHAKESPEARE
Brilliant? That? An awful mess, a joke,
With empty words and vain emotions, quite
Breathtaking in its whole stupidity.

Shakespeare leaves audience and runs on to stage,
where he buttonholes leading actor.

LEADING ACTOR
Why, my fine young feller-
me-lad, we could do with
a sprightly -

SHAKESPEARE
Enough of that.

What means this froth and pother
That dares to show itself upon our stage,
Such sound and fury signifying naught
But vanity and hollow vacancy?

LEADING ACTOR
Oh. So you think you could do better, do you?

SHAKESPEARE
Sirrah, I could. I'd write you such a play
To make the seat and centre point
Of all your feelings shake and sigh and shout
With ecstasy and wild abandonment,
Would freeze your -

LEADING ACTOR
All right, I get the point. I want a two
hour play about King
Henry VI finished ready
to put on in the theatre
at Shoreditch by next
Saturday afternoon.
Got that?

SHAKESPEARE

Indeed I have. I'll write you such a play
To make the rafters ring with cries of joy
And be the first of many that will bring
The whole of England to your theatre fine.

LEADING ACTOR

Well, as long as you know. Then ho! for London, fame
and fortune for us all.

EXEUNT OMNES

Or he might have been in London already...

Chapter 4

The Big World Outside

Now William's on his way to London, what will he find outside Stratford?

A very strange place indeed. England was changing fast.

How?

For hundreds of years things were settled. People knew their place. Peasants were at the bottom, then tradesmen, then knights, then barons. Then came the king. After him was the Pope. Then it was angels and archangels all the way up to God. God made it that way. Binding everything together was the Church. Until now.

Why now?

Two hundred years before, Barons started rebelling against their kings, putting them off their thrones and putting other barons on. There were civil wars like the Wars of the Roses about who should be king. There were peasants' revolts.

The Bible was put into English and other languages, not just Latin.

Printing was invented. More people could read – more had books. They began thinking. TERRIBLE. You could be burnt at the stake for that. But perhaps the world was round, perhaps it moved round the Sun and not the Sun round it – perhaps, perhaps, perhaps...

Starting in Italy and spreading through Europe, artists made pictures and statues, wrote poems, and music for their beauty and meaning, not just to praise God.

Yes, the world was on the move.

What happened next?

Henry VIII, Elizabeth's father, became seriously fed up with Catherine of Aragon, his first wife. He asked the Pope for a divorce. The Pope said "No!" very loudly. Henry said, "Then tough. I'll have my own Church." So started the Church of England. Henry got rid of all the monasteries and took their land and riches. Now he was Head of the Church.

But heaven help anybody who didn't join it. Now the beheadings and burnings started. Henry didn't start his new Church so people could think for themselves. Catholics who didn't change were called "Recusants". They hid. Their priests, if they were caught, were hanged or beheaded.

Henry did a lot of that, did he?

He did, to keep the Catholics quiet.

But Henry forgot – if you break something once, you can break it again into even smaller pieces. People were glad there was no more Pope – but why have Henry's Church either? Some gave up God altogether – atheists. Some wanted to go to God direct, without any priests. All truth was in the Bible which they could read now it had been turned into English. Who needed more?

Thus came the PURITANS. They thought music, poetry and especially plays were SINFUL AND EVIL. Also, Puritans were often rich, as they worked hard, building up big businesses.

Watch out for them, Shakespeare. They could cause you a lot of bother.

So what did the Catholics do about it?

Not much. They waited for Henry to die. Then, when he did – wonderful. His first daughter, Mary Tudor, became Queen. She was still Catholic. The beheadings and burnings went on.

BUT NOW IT WAS THE OTHER WAY ROUND. Then Mary died. Elizabeth's turn.

Ah, Good Queen Bess! I bet she was really nice to everybody

Oh, no she wasn't. She could execute anyone she didn't like –they could be Catholics, atheists, traitors (otherwise known as "anyone she fell out with"). She could:

a) Hang them

b) Throw them in boiling water. Or oil

c) Press them to death between huge millstones

d) Hang, draw and quarter them

e) Burn them alive at the stake

f) Behead them (aristocrats only: they felt quite privileged)

Well, not her personally. But she knew some men who could.

447

Was that the lot?

Yes. Though when Guy Fawkes was sentenced to death in 1606 (Elizabeth was dead, but James carried on the good work) a special committee was set up to think of a REALLY AMUSING NEW WAY to kill him. But they couldn't, so they had to settle for boring old hanging, drawing and quartering after all.

Any more?

Isn't that enough? Shakespeare was setting off through a **very interesting country.**

Chapter 5

Plagues, Plays and Puritans

So what sort of city did William come to?

Not a bit like London today, for a start. Instead of six million
people sprawled over miles and miles, there were about 200,000
squashed in the square mile behind the old Roman walls and a
few suburbs beyond. If you went north to Islington and
Tottenham, you'd be deep in the countryside. If you walked across
old London Bridge between its three floors of shops to the south
bank you'd come to Bankside and Southwark – and then nothing
else except wide, wild Kent and Surrey.

Inside the walls were narrow crisscrossing streets, churches on
nearly every corner, rows of shops, tall timbered houses, great

palaces, grimy hovels and a river chock full of ships, with sails and masts nearly as high as the spire of old St Paul's cathedral.

What about Queen Elizabeth?

She wasn't daft. She lived at Whitehall. This was outside the walls.

What else was inside the walls?

A city council of merchants, craftsmen – and the dreaded PURITANS, giving Shakespeare and the actors a lot of bother.

Why did they give Shakespeare bother?

They thought plays were vain shows in which people forgot their duty to God and only thought about themselves. The theatre was a place of terrible sin which the Bible forbade. They really worried about the sins of their fellow men. And they had a lot to worry about.

Anything more?

Of course. Smell. Stink. Sewage running down the streets. Riots and murders. And above all:

PLAGUE.

Not just any old disease, but real, deadly, killer plague.

It started with nasty boils and finished with you being tipped into a big pit and covered with lime. Some people thought it was brought by the fleas on rats which came to England in ships.

But didn't the council know what the cause was and do something about it?

Not really. The Puritan Council still thought plague came as a punishment for people's sins. Most sinful of all, of course, was the theatre. Not just sinful. TERRIBLE.

So they banned all theatres within the walls.

But if nobody dared go to plays, what was the point of Shakespeare coming all that way to act in them?

Who said they daren't go? They *loved* plays. Besides this Council only ruled *within* the walls. They couldn't stop what went on just outside. So that's where the theatres were, to the north, round Shoreditch and to the south, in Southwark. That's where the actors acted their plays.

All right, who were the actors?

They were the servants of aristocrats. If they didn't have the name of a lord, they were vagabonds and put in prison. Shakespeare was in Lord Derby's troupe. Later, Lord Derby was made Lord Chamberlain by Queen Elizabeth. So Shakespeare ended up with The Lord Chamberlain's Men. It sounded good. Nobody could touch them now, not even the puritans. So they thought.

What were the theatres like?

Small, made of wood and plaster with stages in the open air. No lighting, so plays were put on in the afternoon. No scenery: you used your imagination.

When Macbeth says,

"... *Light thickens and the crow*
Makes wing to the rooky wood.
Good things of day begin to droop and drowse
While night's black agents to their preys do rouse,"

the audience needed no dimmed lighting to imagine the scene.

Sounds useless to me.

Not at all. That's why the words were so important. The plays were fast, with no pauses for scenes to be changed. Characters talked to themselves a lot.

That sounds mad. Were they?

Anything but. That's how we know who they are, what they think, what they feel. These soliloquies are the most memorable things in Shakespeare. Who do you think Hamlet thought was listening when he says:

"To be or not to be: that is the question..."?

Nobody. Except the audience, of course. (Though in this case, he was wrong. People were listening behind the curtains.

Afterwards, they decided Hamlet really must be mad. They were wrong too.)

So did Shakespeare start writing straight away?

He would have acted first, and learnt what went on. He wasn't a bad actor – but he wasn't great, either. So he started writing plays – and soon learnt that trade as well. He got more and more popular. By the time he wrote *Richard III* and *Romeo and Juliet*, everyone knew he was *good*.

So everything was great now, was it?

Well, no, actually.

Chapter 6

Poems, Patrons and more Plague

In 1593, the Plague came worse than ever. At last the Council got their way. They closed down all the theatres. The actors had to go out on the road again.

So there was poor William with no theatres in which to put his plays on and no actors to act them. What did he do?

Did he:

a) Say *"I'm fed up with this. I should never have come to London in the first place. I'm off home to Stratford."*

b) Say, *"I'm through with plays. I'll write stories instead and be a great novelist. Pity television isn't invented yet, I could have written for that. Or gone to Hollywood."*

c) Say, *"I know, I'll just get a job like everyone else."*

Well, what do you think?

Is it a)?

Sort of. He was definitely *very* fed up. And he did go back to Stratford a lot, to see his family, help them when things were hard and buy land and property to come back to one day in the future.

Is it b)?

No. There was no such thing as a novelist. Nobody wrote novels for nearly two hundred years. Besides, not many people could read. That's one reason why theyloved plays. But if there *had* been TV – William Shakespeare would have been on the screen every night, writing scripts for *Eastenders, The Bill,* you name it.

Just think about it. Shakespeare wrote for money, nothing else. He'd have ended up writing Hollywod blockbusters.

Oi, YE!

Was it c)?

No it wasn't. Why not? I don't know. It just wasn't, that's all.

But surely he must have done something?

Yes, he did. He sat down and wrote a letter. It might have said something like this:

> Dear Mr Wriothesley,
>
> Here is a pome wot I have rote. It is my latest opus and I opus as how you like it.
>
> Hoping this finds you as it leaves me at present,
> i.e. in the pink,
>
> W Shaxpur

This is **NOT** actually the letter that Shakespeare wrote. But it's what he meant.

Why did he do it? And who was Mr Wriothesley?

Shakespeare couldn't write novels, but he *could* write poetry. It was very popular with aristocrats, people round Queen Elizabeth's court, young lawyers and the like.

If Shakespeare wanted to make a living from writing today, he'd be paid by a publisher. Or he might get a grant to keep writing from the Arts Council. But not then. No, the way to do it was by getting a *patron*. Other poets did. So Shakespeare did too.

So what was a patron? A rich aristocrat who liked poetry, and especially poems dedicated to him. He might pay for a few more.

And Mr Wriothesley? Henry Wriothesley was only 19. But he was already the Earl of Southampton and as rich as they come. Queen Elizabeth thought the world of him. Ideal.

Or so Shakespeare thought. Sadly, in the end, he turned out to be the very worst choice Shakespeare could have made.

So William sent Henry a poem. Why should Henry be so pleased with it?

Because it was really rather a naughty piece of verse. It was a long story – *Venus and Adonis.* It was about this innocent young

lad who is fancied by the Goddess of Love herself. He ends up dead. She, being a goddess, doesn't.

Henry liked it. So William sent him another one – *The Rape of Lucrece* – in which Lucrece is fancied by ancient Romans.

Henry liked that too. So William sent him some sonnets. And then some more sonnets. And then even more. In the end he wrote 154 sonnets.

ONE HUNDRED AND FIFTY-FOUR. Yes, Shakespeare liked sonnets. So, it seemed, did Henry Wriothesley. Yes, sonnets were their bag all right. Sonnets were fantastic. Long live SONNETS.

Are there any questions so far? Ask me now, because I won't be stopping again.

Chapter 7

Some Answers

Yes?

What is a sonnet?

A poem exactly fourteen lines long. They'd been going a long time and were very popular just then. Shakespeare liked them because he could pack a lot of meaning into a short space.

He could write lines which have never been forgotten:

Lilies that fester smell as rank as weeds

He could be regretful and melancholy, thinking of what used to be:

Bare ruined choirs where late the sweet birds sang

He could be mocking about some mysterious woman:

My mistress' eyes are nothing like the sun...
If hairs be wires, black wires grow on her head.

Who was she? Did she exist? No-one knows. No wonder she's called *"The Dark Lady of the Sonnets."*

Did Anne Hathaway know about this Dark Lady?

I don't know. But if she didn't exist, Anne wouldn't have worried too much. Don't ask me what she would have thought if the Lady was real. If black wires grew on her head, I doubt if Anne would have been too bothered.

Why couldn't Shakespeare spell his own name?

Nobody could spell their own names. Or anything else. Spellings kept changing all the time. They spelt words the way they sounded. It was printers who got fed up with this and insisted words were spelt the same all the time.

So who was this Robert Greene who hated Shakespeare that we met at the beginning?

He wrote plays. He had been to University and he had a lot of friends like Kit Marlowe, Thomas Kyd, John Lyly and George Peele who also wrote plays. They were called 'The University Wits'.

They thought that because they'd had such a great education they were the only ones who could write plays. They didn't think mere actors could possibly do anything like that.

But after Shakespeare and a few others like Ben Jonson started, plays were written by actors themselves, for their own companies. And, sadly for Robert Greene, the plays that William wrote before Greene died were loved by everyone. *William was top playwright!*

After the plague, the University Wits never wrote plays again. Greene was dead and Marlowe – who Shakespeare was friendly with and admired – was killed in a fight in a pub. An accident?

Never. It was a put-up job. Marlowe was a secret agent for the government.

So how did Shakespeare end up playing for Walsall?

I did say it was *much, much* later, didn't I? Craig Shakespeare was a midfield player for Walsall only a few years ago.

'Shakespeare' was once a common name in the midlands and is still around today. If William's only son Hamnet hadn't died in 1596 when he was only 10, there might have been more now.

Why wasn't Henry Wriothesley a good choice as a patron?

Wait and see.

Chapter 8

Shakespeare in Love –
sort of...

Well, the plague went away. For a while, anyway. So the theatres could start up again. And on came the plays – play after play.

Think of them: *Romeo and Juliet, Richard II, Taming of the Shrew, Midsummer Night's Dream, Merchant of Venice*. And more besides. All completely different. All making people flock into Shoreditch and the theatre.

But Shakespeare NEVER MADE UP A SINGLE STORY OF HIS OWN.

What do you mean? Did he just copy the plays out?

No, definitely not. He found old stories from poems, ballads, legends, history books – and turned them into what he wanted. That was his great secret. He could take something old and forgotten and make it marvellous. Beside, he just didn't have time to think up new plots.

Ah, life on the stage. Fit to wear anybody out. Shakespeare was writing and acting and producing from dawn to dusk. He composed his plays very quickly – so that when he was dead, Ben Jonson wrote, *"He never blotted a line."* But Ben himself worked slowly and thought William would have done better if he had as well. So he added, *"Would he had blotted a thousand."* By "blotted", he meant "crossed out and altered." Cheeky devil.

Did Shakespeare never get any time off, then?
Yes, he did.

Did he have any friends?
Yes, he did.

Who were they?

There were mainly the other actors in his company – Richard Burbage, John Heminges, Augustine Phillips and the clowns Will Kemp and Robert Armin. And then there was Ben Jonson.

Tell us about them

Burbage took all the big leading parts. He was Romeo, Brutus in *Julius Caesar,* Hamlet, Macbeth, Othello, King Lear, Antony, Prospero in *The Tempest.* As Burbage got older, so – more or less – did the characters he played. He had red hair and a terrible temper, so they say. Heminges could do most things.

After William died, he and another actor, Henry Condell, made sure all the plays were printed. That's the only reason we still know about them...

Augustine Phillips did the music for the plays.

Will Kemp was a great comedian. Once, he *danced* from London to Norwich. Why? He must have been sponsored. Or very fit. Or mad.

Robert Armin was very small and had long arms. He could tie himself up in knots. He was a *riot!*

Ben Jonson acted and also wrote plays. William acted in at least two – a funny one called *Every Man in his Humour* and a Roman tragedy called *Sejanus.* Ben used to be a bricklayer and William got him started in the theatre.

So were these theatre folk William's only friends?

Well...

Go on, tell us

Oh, all right. It's said that once he and Richard Burbage were after the same girl. Richard had arranged to see her one night and said she'd know who it was because he'd come as Richard III, the play he'd just been acting in. But when he knocked at the door and whispered,

"Shhh... it's Richard III,"

the window opened, Shakespeare looked out and said,

"Sorry. William the Conqueror got here first."

Is that true?

If it is, DON'T TELL ANNE HATHAWAY.

Is there anything more you think you ought to tell us?

Not that I know of.

So Bill was a bit naughty when he was in London and miles away from Anne, was he?

Wouldn't you like to know! Wouldn't I, as well. Wouldn't everybody!

But I guess we never will.

Chapter 9

Into the Globe

The century was nearly over. Things were going well for the Lord Chamberlain's Men.

Or were they?

Actually, they were in a mess. The theatre was nearly falling down. The man who owned the land was called Giles Allen. He was a puritan and deep down wanted the actors out. So he put the rent up so high they couldn't afford it.

So what did they do? Did they:

a) Break into Giles Allen's house while he was asleep, find the lease, alter it so it said *Rent – 5 pence a year,* forge his signature and break out again?

b) Say "Plays aren't worth all this aggro. Let's go and live in the country and commune with nature?"

c) Steal the theatre?

Well, **a)** might not have been a bad idea. They just can't have had anybody who could forge his signature.

People who were wise never did **b)** in those days. Unless they were lords with big estates. If they weren't they'd probably be peasants. For them, the country was hard and horrible. And nobody in his right mind would try communing with nature.

So they did **c)**.

Don't be stupid. How can you steal a theatre?

Well, they did.

They had found some spare land on the south side of the river. The winter of 1598 was very cold. The Thames had frozen over. They chose a night when it was snowing hard, so nobody would be around to watch, their footprints would be hidden and they wouldn't be seen through the falling flakes. Then they took the theatre to pieces and loaded all the wooden beams on carts. A carpenter called Peter Streete told them how to do it. Then they

Part 1
of
ye
GLOBE

guided the horses and carts along the icy streets from Shoreditch to Southwark.

Did they take the carts across the frozen Thames?

Probably not or the theatre might have ended at the bottom of the river. More likely they led the horses across London Bridge.

Peter Streete rebuilt the theatre in 28 days. They called it The Globe.

It was – and still is – just about the most famous theatre in the world.

What did Giles Allen think when he woke up and found the theatre gone?

I should think he was furious. But there wasn't a lot he could do about it. He owned the land, not what was on it. Besides, who'd want to pull the Globe down, take it back to Shoreditch and put it up again?

No, once the flag was flying to show a play was on and the audiences were streaming across the river, nobody would dare to touch the great Globe, most popular place in London.

Chapter 10

"Sad stories about the death of kings."

Once there was a rather feeble king of England. He was kicked off his throne by the other nobles. This was nearly 200 years before William wrote his first play.

So what? – you may ask. Well, William wrote a play about him. Richard II. In it, King Richard says:

> *"For God's sake let us sit upon the ground*
> *And tell sad stories of the*
> *death of kings."*

Er.....is the ground too wet to sit on?

This was not a very clever thing to say, because while he was telling stories, this man called Henry Bolingbroke was actually DOING THE BUSINESS. He had himself crowned, Richard locked up in a castle and then murdered.

People loved this play. All except Queen Elizabeth. She *hated* it. Surprise, surprise.

> # INTERRUPTION.
> *Very interesting, but you still haven't told us why Henry Wriothesley wasn't a good patron for Shakespeare to choose.*

Your wait is over.

Henry W's best friend was the Earl of Essex. Once upon a time, Elizabeth rather fancied Essex – until she found he was plotting about who should succeed her. Guess who he had in mind. Why, Essex, of course.

To get rid of him Elizabeth put him in charge of an army sent to squash a rebellion in Ireland.

Essex asked Henry W to be second-in-command. Off they sailed.

THEY MADE A PIG'S EAR OF IT.

So they had to come back to England complete failures.

What did they do then? Did they:

a) Go to Elizabeth and say, *"We messed up. Sorry, Liz. But we've bought you a bottle of duty-free Irish whiskey and a bunch of shamrock to make up for it."*

b) Pretend they'd really won, make two soldiers dress up in green, kneel in front of her and say, *"Sure, Your Majesty, and aren't you the finest queen in the world, at all, at all, begorrah. Have a shillelagh."*

c) Realise there was no way out, start a rebellion, kick Elizabeth off the throne and let Essex be king instead.

No, it doesn't matter that myself, I'd try **a)**. They tried **c)**.

They laid their plans carefully.

Right. Put yourself in their position. You want to start a rebellion. What do you do?
Do you:

a) Get millions of people on your side with lots of propaganda so everyone thinks you're right and rallies to your cause?

b) Recruit a huge army which can crush the ruling power with no trouble?

c) Plan a campaign which will carry you through the whole country and make the capital city and the government all yours?

d) Get some actors in a theatre to put on a play?

Myself, I'd do **a)**, **b)** AND **c)**. But Essex and Henry W, they thought they'd get away with just doing **d)**. ...Mad.

So they went to Shakespeare's company and asked for a play to be put on specially the day before the rebellion was due to start.

Maybe this is what happened then.

SCENE:
ᴛᴅᴇ ɢʟᴏʙᴇ ᴛᴅᴇᴀᴛʀᴇ

Shakespeare stands on the stage.
He is thinking about writing a new play.

---

shakespeare

I know. I'll call it Hamlet. I wonder if I could nip across
to Denmark and soak up a bit of atmosphere.

Enter Essex and Henry Wriothesley

henry w

I say, Bill, my old mate, how about putting on a play
just to please a friend? A sort of request time?

shakespeare

Of course we will. Anything for you, Henry. How
about 'Twelfth Night'? A few good laughs there. Or
'Romeo and Juliet'? Never a dry eye in the house.

essex

None of them. What we want is Richard II.

shakespeare

What, that old thing? We haven't done it for years.
Wouldn't you rather have Henry V? Real patriotic
stuff, that.

henry w

It's Richard II or the deal's off. But if you do what we want when we want, we'll pay you 40 shillings extra.

shakespeare (amazed)

40 shillings?

essex

Yes, mate, 40 shillings. The time will come, give or take a bit of inflation, when you won't get paid that much for a Coronation Street script.

shakespeare

Well, if you put it like that, we might see our way to...

essex (rather threateningly)

You'd better.

henry w (Taps finger on side of nose)

Say no more, squire. Nudge, nudge, wink, wink, know what I mean?

EXEUNT OMNES

Well, perhaps not quite like that. But Shakespeare's actors definitely did *Richard II* for the Earl of Essex the day before the rebellion for 40 shillings more than they usually got.

The day of the performance came. The theatre was packed. All went well. Then the Duke of York said: *"...plume plucked Richard.....his high sceptre yields/ To the possession of thy royal hand.../ And long live Henry, fourth of that name."*
Henry Bolingbroke answered: *"In God's name I'll ascend the royal throne."*

The audience started shouting, screaming and stamping their feet.

essex

Ah, that's what I like to hear.

henry w

That Henry Bolingbroke knew what he was doing all right.

essex's second best friend,

whoever he was

About time we had a proper king ourselves, not the stupid woman with too much make-up on that we've got now.

shakespeare

(mutters to other actors) Do you think we're doing the right thing here?

Well they very nearly weren't.

Next day came the revolution. Did Essex and Henry win? No. What a shame for them that **a)**, **b)** and **c)** hadn't occurred to either Essex or Henry. Or Essex's second best friend. As a result, they didn't get very far. They were captured and brought before Elizabeth.

Elizabeth

I always knew Essex men were revolting. Take them away.

Where to? A big place by the river Thames with Beefeaters and ravens, beginning with **T.** Here Essex met a man holding something beginning with **A.** Soon, he lost something beginning with **H.**

What was it?

Well, he couldn't blow his nose. But it wasn't his handkerchief.
She took pity on Henry W and showed mercy. She put him in the Tower for life and took all his possessions away.

He probably said as the jailer turned the key.
I have no idea what happened to Essex's second best friend.

So what about Shakespeare and the actors?

They said at Essex's trial.

They got away with it. The night before Essex was beheaded, they even acted a play especially for Elizabeth.

They knew which side their bread was buttered. In those days, you had to.

Chapter 11

Any more Questions?

Yes, there are.

You said Burbage was Romeo, Macbeth and Antony. So who played Juliet, Lady Macbeth and Cleopatra?

Well, they weren't women, for a start. Women were barred from acting. No, they were boys whose voices hadn't broken.

So that was how you started a career in the theatre?

Not necessarily. Shakespeare didn't. And a lot of boys ended up in all-boys' companies, run by St Paul's cathedral and the Chapel Royal. So everybody thought they were great – but they only became grown-up actors if they were too poor to do anything else.

They acted in the city, at Blackfriars, in the warm and dry in an indoor theatre, with lots of lighting and special effects. Shakespeare hated them!

You said at the beginning that William was taken to the Miracle Plays in Coventry. How can you possibly know that?

Well, I don't really. But it is a very good guess, and here's why.

There's a Coventry play in which King Herod appears and slaughters the Innocents to make sure Jesus is dead and can't be king. In it he gets very, very angry. The stage direction says:

> # Here, Herod rages on the pageant and in the street also.

So Herod was screaming his head off!

Back to *Hamlet*. Shakespeare's telling the players not to shriek and shout their words, because it *"Out-herods Herod." Convinced?*

No, not really. How do you know that?
Stick around and I'll tell you.

It had better be more convincing than the last lot.
I'll do my best.

Chapter 12

Feeling rotten

About the time he wrote *Hamlet*, Shakespeare does not seem to have been very happy. His plays are strange and gloomy. They are full of disgust – at himself and the rest of the world. He tries to write comedies, like *All's Well That Ends Well* and *Measure for Measure*. But where they're funny, they're also slightly sick and the characters are weird. He wrote his greatest play – *Hamlet* – at this time. It's a tragedy. But it's a lot more as well.

Hamlet is told by his father's ghost how he was poisoned by his brother Claudius, who then married Hamlet's mother, Gertrude. Hamlet vows revenge.

But he can't bring himself to do it. He has to work out a terrible problem in his mind. He drives his girlfriend, Ophelia, to suicide. When he does kill Claudius, it's a terrible mess. Hamlet ends up dead as well and so does nearly everyone else except his only friend Horatio and Fortinbras, Prince of Norway who leads in his army at the end. Perhaps an invasion is just as well. As Hamlet says:

"Something is rotten in the state of Denmark."

But what? And where, and how, do you find it?
Was something rotten in the state of Shakespeare as well? Was something on his mind? Was it...

"Murder most foul?"

Perhaps something like this had just happened, when Shakespeare was buying New Place in Stratford.

SCENE:
THE OFFICE OF FLOGGIT AND GAZUMPEM, ELIZABETHAN ESTATE AGENTS IN STRATFORD.

Enter Shakespeare and Mr Floggit

FLOGGIT

So, William, you're interested in buying New Place.
Very desirable property, if I may say so.

SHAKESPEARE

I've known it ever since I was a child. The nicest house
in the town. I always hoped I might one day have
enough money to buy it for my family.

FLOGGIT

So you don't worry about some of the things that
happened in it.

SHAKESPEARE

I've been away a long time. You'll have to remind me.

FLOGGIT

Well, you couldn't remember the first one It was in 1563, the year before you were born. A William Bott lived there.

Nasty piece of work if ever there was one. He wanted all his rich son-in-law's possessions for himself. So do you know what he did?

SHAKESPEARE

No, but I can see you're going to tell me.

FLOGGIT

You're dead right, I am. First, this Bott forged some papers which said he'd get all his daughter's husband's possessions if she died without having children. Then guess what he did.

SHAKESPEARE

I'm afraid I'm getting a pretty good idea.

FLOGGIT

You're right. He poisoned his own daughter to get all the property.

Shakespeare does not answer, but starts thinking deeply

FLOGGIT
I haven't finished yet. The next to live there was another William, Underhill this time. He was poisoned as well. Do you know who by?

SHAKESPEARE
I don't think I want to.

FLOGGIT
By Fulk, his own son. That's who.

SHAKESPEARE *(to himself)*
A father murders his daughter, a son murders his father. What can be worse than murders within families? I'm not sure I want to buy this house after all.

FLOGGIT
Oh, don't take any notice of me. I'm always one for a joke. Just don't let it prey on your mind, that's all.

EXEUNT OMNES

Well, was it true? Yes, it seems certain that it was.

Was it knowing about these murders in his own house which made him so unhappy? Or was he feeling that way already and these murders merely made it worse? With all these murders inside families, Hamlet's Elsinore castle is like New Place must have been when Bott and the Underhills lived there.

Or perhaps there were things which went even deeper.

Such as?

Plague and bad harvests. Life was hard in England. Rebellion and riot were near. A friend of the Shakespeares, Richard Quiney, was elected as town bailiff. Sir Edward Greville, Lord of the Manor, didn't want him to be bailiff. So he sent his men to beat him up. They smashed him round the head with cudgels and killed him.

Nobody was ever punished for it.

"For who would bear the whips and scorns of time,
The oppressor's wrong, the proud man's contumely?"

says Hamlet. By "contumely," he meant "abuse" or "humiliation".
So very much was wrong – terrible things happening in Stratford while England was nearly starving.

All except the rich. They were very rich. They'd got it, they flaunted it and they meant to keep it. Doesn't it sound familiar?

Besides, William was still grieving for his only son Hamnet not long dead. All his hopes now lay with his daughters, Judith and Susanna.

And what was happening in London? Was he having trouble with that mysterious Dark Lady of the Sonnets?

Who knows?

Chapter 13

Goodbye Elizabeth – Hello James

If only Essex and Henry W could have held out for a couple of years. Elizabeth died in 1603.

Who was to succeed her? She left no children. England would be ruled by a stranger. This was terrible. Especially when they found out who.

King James. A Scotsman. Scotland was 'The old enemy'. Wars had been fought between England and Scotland and there would

be more yet. Scotland was a separate country with its own king and James was already King James VI there. Now he was to be King James I of England as well.

Worse. *He was the son of Mary Queen of Scots and Elizabeth had had his mother's head cut off.*

It did not bode well.

But in the end, thing's weren't too bad. James seemed to like the actors anyway. Soon Shakespeare's company changed its name. Henceforth, they were to be **THE KING'S MEN.** So not everything in William's life was doom and gloom.

What could they do to show the king how pleased they were?

Why, act him a play, of course. So William wrote one specially.

MACBETH
The unlucky play.
Even today, actors won't call it by its name. So it's –

The Scottish Play

It's murderous.
Dark.
Flowing with blood.
Supernatural.

And, for James, very good listening. For while the witches tell Macbeth:
"Thou shalt be king hereafter"

they tell Banquo:
"Thou shalt get kings, though thou shalt be none."

When Macbeth has murdered King Duncan, who is a guest in his own castle, he knows he must get rid of Banquo. So he has him murdered. But Banquo comes to Macbeth's feast even though:

"...safe in a ditch he lies
With twenty trenched gashes on his head."

However, his son Fleance has got away and the accusing, mocking ghost marks the beginning of the end for Macbeth.

Yes, Shakespeare knew what he was doing. James was descended from Banquo and Fleance, so *Macbeth* is a play about when his family started being kings.

Clever old William. Never missed a trick if he could help it.

Chapter 14

William's Last Years
in London

Life at the Globe was as good as it would get for the King's Men.

But was it for Shakespeare?

King Lear is about an old man and his three daughters. Lear is king of England and divides his kingdom between them. But first they must tell him how much they love him. Goneril and Regan say how wonderful he is. Great. But what does Cordelia, his favourite, say?

"*Nothing, my Lord.*"
"*Nothing will come of nothing. Speak again,*" says Lear.

But Cordelia repeats: she loves her father as much as a daughter should: no more, no less.

So start all Lear's troubles and the most harrowing tragedy of all that Shakespeare or anyone else ever wrote. The end is so painful that after Shakespeare died, nobody could bear to read it, act it or watch it. So the play was given a happy ending by someone else, which stayed until 1838.

But it's only a play. Why should Shakespeare be unhappy?

Was Shakespeare writing about himself, what he hoped for, what he feared? He had two daughters and he loved them. But did they love him? Did they worry him? Susanna was his favourite. But she was headstrong. However, when she married Dr John Hall, Shakespeare was very pleased. He really liked him. What about Judith? One day, she would upset her father very much. But perhaps not yet.

These terrible tragedies don't sound a barrel of laughs.

You're right. I wonder if this is what people thought?

"What's on today then?"

"King Lear. This old king gives his country away, dies and so does his favourite daughter. Lear's friend, the old duke of Gloucester, has his eyes gouged out. There's hardly anyone left at the end who's not dead. Do you fancy it?"

"What's the weather like?"

"Rain and wind. The Thames will be rough when we cross it. That thatched roof on the Globe will drip water all over me again."

"What do you say? Give it a miss?"

"OK. Let's hope it gets better for next week. It's Othello. He's a

big bloke who gets so jealous he puts a pillow over his wife's face and suffocates her."

"Charming. I bet we have to stand in the snow to watch that."

Yes, you had to be tough to watch Shakespeare's plays.

The King's Men probably thought the same about acting outdoors in winter. What could they do? Those rotten boys' companies had warm indoor theatres. Until they went broke. At once, the King's Men bought the Blackfriars Theatre.

And Shakespeare started writing completely different plays for it.

Romances. Fantasies. Lots of music, lots of spectacle, lots of lighting effects. They can have these now they're indoors. *Pericles, Cymbeline, A Winter's Tale*. And, above all – *The Tempest*.

Families are reunited. Lost children are found. But all's not well.

There's trouble in them – King Leontes in *A Winter's Tale* is jealous and wants to kill his wife. In *The Tempest*, Caliban is a strange creature living on the island, who says to the magician Prospero:

"You taught me language, and the consequence is
I know how to curse."

Perhaps Shakespeare was tired of London and plays. Perhaps he wanted to look after his family more. Perhaps he'd made enough money. After *The Tempest*, in 1610 he left London and went back to Stratford. *"Our revels now are ended,"* says Prospero, and *The Tempest* ends with Prospero saying,

"Now my charms are all o'erthrown,
And what strength I have's mine own."

It's as if Shakespeare is saying, "I've written you all these plays over the years but now I'm tired and I'm just giving up."

That was it. Except for when they got him to help someone else, **NO MORE PLAYS FOR WILLIAM.**

Chapter 15

The End

Didn't he get fed up, back in that dead-and-alive place?

It doesn't seem so. Besides, he kept going down to London to see how things were going. But he had a lot to do in Stratford. He had property to look after, a family to see off into the grown-up world, troubles all around as big to him here as anything in London.

And that was it, was it?

Not completely. He wrote part of *Henry VIII* with his friend John Fletcher. He helped in a play called *Cardenio*, now lost.

A missing play by Shakespeare? Why can't someone find it?

Wouldn't they love to! It would be beyond any price now.

What did he do in London when he went there?

In 1613 he bought a house there, near the Blackfriars Theatre. But in the same year – DISASTER!

Go on. What was it?

The roof of the Globe should never have been thatched. The King's Men were playing *Henry VIII*, a cannon was fired on stage and a spark caught the straw.

End of the Globe, a pile of ash.

'ere... do you feel hot?

That cannon's deafened me... It's a quarter to four.

So what did the King's Men do?

Built another Globe Theatre at once. This time, the roof was tiled.

And William helped, of course.

No. It seems he didn't. He saw the smoking heap, said, *"Enough is enough"*, sold his theatre shares and got out quick.

Was he sad?

Who can tell. He had enough to do at home anyway. Judith was seeing a lot of Thomas Quiney. Compared with his father, who was murdered by the Lord of the Manor's men, Thomas was useless and *a rat*. But nothing could be done to stop it – in 1515 they were married.

Why was he useless?

Because everything he tried went wrong. He tried selling wine and messed it up. He tried selling tobacco and lost money. He needed money badly and tried very hard to get it off Shakespeare.

Why was he a rat?

Because after he and Judith were married, he went around with other women.

What did Shakespeare think of this?

What do you think? When he made his will, he left things to Judith

> *"and any such husband as she may have".*

So he wouldn't accept that Thomas was married to her! Even when the lawyer nearly wrote

> *"son-in-law,"*

it's crossed out and

> *"My daughter Judith"*

written over it. So much for Thomas.

And to his wife Anne went

> *"My second-best bed with all the furniture."*

Generous or what?

Who got most in the will?
Susanna, his favourite daughter.

Why was he making a will?

Because it was March 1616 and he was ill.

What was the matter with him?

Some say Ben Jonson and another actor turned up to see him, they all went out drinking and William got so drunk he took a fever or had a stroke.

Some even say Thomas Quiney, because William wouldn't help him, murdered him by giving him poison.

But what's most likely is this. That stream flowing past New Place was very unhealthy and there wasn't much in the way of loos and clean running water in 1616. Shakespeare caught typhoid fever and once you got that, you just had to wait until it killed you.

So on April 23rd, 1616, the same day as he was probably born 52 years before, he died.

But his story had hardly started.

Chapter 16

So what have we got?

What do you mean, his story had hardly started?

When he died all those years ago, what do you think his last words were?

Were they:

a) "Why do you keep on staring at me, Thomas?"

b) "Pen and paper, quick! I've just thought of a brilliant new play. It's going to be the best thing I've ever done."

c) "I do hope they choose me to be 'Man of the Millenium.'"

I haven't a clue.
Neither have I. But I do know they weren't **c)**. He never thought he was going to be famous. He believed he was just someone who'd earned good money writing plays for his company.

But now – all over the world his plays are acted, in every language, in every style. All the time they end up saying *more* to us, *more* and *more* and *MORE.* He's the biggest draw for tourists

any country can ever have had. He's driven kids at school mad because everyone has to read him. Some think it's boring.

But it's not. It's wonderful. Why?

That would need another ten books!

ABOUT THE AUTHORS

MICK GOWAR

Napoleon

Julius Caesar

Mick Gowar has over 100 books for children published to date, including collections of poetry, novels, graphic novels, picture books and short stories. Mick has also been involved in a variety of broadcast media. He frequently tours schools and other venues to give talks and performances of his work, or to lead workshops.

DENNIS HAMLEY

William Shakespeare

Charles Darwin

Dennis Hamley has written over sixty books for children, both fiction and non-fiction. His fiction includes *The War and Freddy*, which was shortlisted for the Smarties Prize, *Hare's Choice*, *Ellen's People* and *Divided Loyalties*. For many years he was a teacher, a trainer of teachers and, before he took early retirement to be a full-time writer, County English Adviser for Hertfordshire. He has two children and five grandchildren and lives with his partner in Oxford.

MARTIN OLIVER

Tutankhamun

Martin Oliver has written many fiction and non-fiction titles for children. He first came face-to-face with Tutankhamun when he was nine years old at an exhibition in London. It was an event that started an interest in all things ancient Egyptian.

VICTORIA PARKER

Victoria Parker read English at Oxford University and has a special interest in history, mythologies and different cultures. Since working for 8 years as a Commissioning Editor of children's books, she has written over 100 non-fiction and fiction titles, for all ages.

WHO AM I?

Joan of Arc